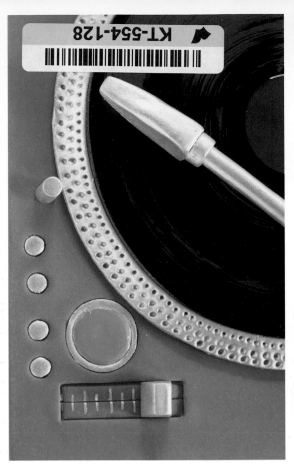

Welcome to Planet Cake

Long before Planet Cake was born, a decorated cake gave me my first real career break. Straight from school and only 18 years old, I was working as a runner in one of Sydney's top stockbroking firms. I ran all over town delivering trading dockets, constantly exhausted and earning a very low wage but seeing it as an opportunity for greater things. After six months that opportunity came when I was invited, along with everyone at the firm, to a 60th birthday party for one of the senior partners. The rumour was that if you could impress a partner, your career would be fast-tracked straight to the trading floor. My delight quickly turned to unease when everyone began discussing their gifts (I can remember through my haze of anxiety that a gold Rolex was mentioned). I could barely afford my rent let alone an extravagant present.

However, I discovered that the senior partner loved Harley Davidson motorbikes, so I decided to make him a very special cake. This cake was crudely designed and poorly executed and I felt sick with embarrassment when I arrived at the party, only to be overwhelmed by his response. My motorbike cake was placed as the party centrepiece, I became the belle of the ball, and from that moment the senior partner took an active interest in my career. It was an amazing lesson in what giving a little time and imagination can achieve in a material world where people can buy anything they want. However, much to the dismay of my family, I left my big break in stockbroking (I found myself reading craft magazines instead of financial reports and spent my lunch hours talking to the florist about her displays for the company foyer rather than networking with clients) and fell, quite by accident, into my dream job.

When I first stumbled across Planet Cake in 2003 it was a tiny little shop located down a Sydney side street and had already been operating virtually unchanged for seven years. The shop was originally established by Margie Carter, a world-class cake decorator who we are fortunate enough to still have at Planet Cake as Artistic Director. The original store was painted electric blue and had a dusty figurine of Astro Boy in the front window and cupids on the walls; in terms of size it was not much bigger than my daughter's bedroom. However, inside was a magical world of cakes. It was this atmosphere of creativity and the exceptional quality of the work that persuaded me to invest in the business and become owner of Planet Cake.

From these modest beginnings we've moved to a much larger production kitchen (in which we've created many 'celebrity' wedding cakes, including that of Nicole Kidman and Keith Urban). Our kitchen also serves as a classroom: we began holding decorating workshops in 2004 and have now taught hundreds of students, and trained and employed many talented cake decorators. We are a true team, with a specialist in every area: novelty, figurines, sugar flowers, piping and wedding cakes. It is the creativity and high-quality techniques of this team that we want to share with you in this book.

The best starting point

Unbelievably, Planet Cake exports from Sydney as far afield as Europe and South America. This is entirely due to the way we set up our cakes and our use of ready-to-roll (RTR) fondant icing, which does not require refrigeration. I constantly receive questions from aspiring decorators wanting to know how we achieve the sharp edges on our cakes, and keep them moist and delicious. If you have ever eaten a dry novelty cake with unpalatable thick icing, then you'll appreciate the method I'm going to show you to avoid that.

Spending the extra time to make sure your cake is perfectly sculpted and covered with a completely smooth layer of chocolate ganache before you ice it allows you to use one layer of thin icing. It is this that will give you the sharp edges and crisp look every cake decorator craves. This book is set out in a specific order so that you spend time learning to ganache and cover a cake perfectly before moving on to the top layer of decorating. This is the same method we use to train students in our kitchen classroom.

Our philosophy is that if you cannot set up your cake properly and cover it expertly then, no matter how brilliant and creative your decorating, the cake will always look clunky and unprofessional, and it will probably taste dry as well. There really is no secret to becoming a great cake decorator other than solid skills in ganaching and covering, an eye for colour and

proportion, practice and patience. In a commercial environment, trainee cake decorators are taught by shape and that is the method we will follow in this book. As a new trainee at Planet Cake you would spend a year focusing on ganaching and covering cakes, mastering increasingly difficult shapes as you advance, and that is how we have set out our chapters. The program is designed so that you will gain different skills and re-enforce techniques already learnt as the cakes become progressively more advanced.

Cupcakes and round cakes are where beginners should start. In these chapters you'll learn the crucial decorating skills that will form the basis of the rest of your learning. Leaping in and decorating a square cake with no prior experience can be a frustrating exercise. The square has a few tricks regarding angles that are much better mastered once you have experience in covering round cakes with RTR icing.

It's very tempting to want to rush into making a groovy-shaped or novelty cake but your results will be much higher (and your stress levels much lower) if you have had prior experience with round and square cakes. So, if you start with cupcakes or round cakes and methodically work through each chapter, you will actually be completing the same training as a trainee at Planet Cake.

Have fun, and enjoy the results.

How to use this book

The first two chapters of this book will provide you with several delicious cake and icing recipes. These are the same cakes that we use at Planet Cake, so we know the recipes work well, the cakes are firm enough to give a good basis for decorating, and they store well. The glossary and equipment pages will give you photographic reference for stocking your kitchen. The techniques chapter will then lead you through the basics of cake decorating, giving you hints and tips and also a section on trouble-shooting when something goes wrong.

Ganache
Have a good look at how we set-up our cakes with ganache to achieve very clean and sharp edges. Ganache also tastes much better than the buttercream that some people use, and the cake keeps for much longer.

RTR icing
At Planet Cake we only use ready-to-roll (RTR) fondant icing, which finishes with a nice satin shine and is very reliable. We always buy this ready made, but if you did want to make your own for some reason see the recipe on page 33. Because we set up the cakes first with a smooth hard layer of ganache that hides any imperfections and gives a perfect foundation, this allows us to use only a thin layer of RTR icing.

Using a pasta machine
One of our 'tricks' at Planet Cake is to use a pasta machine for rolling out icing evenly. If you don't already own a pasta machine, buy a cheap one and you'll find it much easier than the traditional rolling pin. You can even use the spaghetti-making setting to make tassels for the flag cake (page 138).

Using a flexi-scraper
Another useful item you will discover is our flexi-scraper (one of our proudest inventions!). You can make this out of firm plastic so that it is firm but remains flexible (see glossary, page 17). We use the flexi-scraper for buffing and polishing the icing, which is the 'secret' to the sharp edges that give our cakes their professional look.

Storing and transporting your cake
Keep your decorated cake away from water as this will 'burn' the icing and leave it stained. Sunlight will fade the colour of the icing and heat will soften it, so any decorations may melt or droop. However, never put the iced cake in the fridge as the damp environment will make the icing sweat. Store the finished cake in a cake box, putting a non-slip rubber mat under the cake board to prevent the cake moving. To prevent cupcakes from moving, stick them on the cake board with royal icing.

Essential planning and preparation

Planning

Two weeks prior to making your cake, check through the recipe to ensure you have all the materials and ingredients required.

Making and decorating cakes always takes longer than you think, and for an enjoyable experience it is important to be as organised as possible. If you are making a cake for a special event make sure you have all the materials and equipment necessary. Some specialist products or equipment might not always be in stock and may require ordering in advance from a supplier.

Designing

The designs in this book can be followed to the letter or, as you gain more confidence, tailored to your own needs. Once you have learnt the techniques, they are easily adapted. Obviously, the easiest thing to change is the colour palette. However, you can also change the cut-outs or decoration detail, for example the Exploding star cake (page 122) can be easily changed to hearts for Valentine's Day or an engagement party, and the Flag cake (page 138) also works well as the flag of a country or sports team.

Note: Some designs use non-edible elements such as toothpicks or plastic tubing that need removing before the cake is served.

Preparing the work space

I cannot emphasise enough how important it is to prepare your work space before you start. Make sure you have everything you require, including: room in the freezer if you're going to freeze your cake before decorating; adequate bench space and boards; all the equipment and ingredients to hand such as cornflour for lightly dusting the work surface and plastic sheets. RTR icing dries out very quickly and, therefore, always wrap the icing in plastic or, if already rolled, cover it with a plastic sheet.

The three-day rule

The three-day rule is very important. If you want to create a wonderful, professional-looking cake, this is the time that it requires and it is futile (and stressful) to try to hurry it. Cakes that are not given time to cool, or ganache that has not been allowed to set properly will make poor foundations for the rest of the decoration.

Day 1: Bake your basic cake and allow adequate cooling time. Most of our basic cakes (pages 22–7) can be kept for up to a week in an airtight container, or in the freezer for 2 months before decorating.

Day 2: Cut and ganache the cake (page 36) and allow adequate setting time.

Day 3: Decorate the cake.

This is the basic set of equipment you will need to make and decorate cakes. You don't need to buy all these tools at once — you might prefer to start with some simple items, such as a couple of piping tips, which can also be used as circle cutters, and a rolling pin, and then slowly build up your tool box.

Icing equipment

1. Flour shaker
2. Pizza wheel
3. Small knife
4. Large rolling pin
5. Icing smoothers in different sizes
6. Scissors
7. Zip-lock bags
8. Flexi-scraper
9. Turntable (for TV)

Edible decorations and materials

1. Ready-to-roll fondant icing (RTR)
2. Decorating alcohol
3. Tylose powder
4. Colouring paste
5. Florist tape
6. Piping gel
7. Colouring paste
8. Cachous
9. Edible glitter
10. Edible gold dust
11. Instant royal icing
12. Liquid colouring
13. Container for liquids
14. Cornflour

Ganaching tools

1. Plastic jug
2. Cleaning cloth
3. Palette knives
4. Large palette knife
5. Serrated or bread knife
6. Masonite set-up and display cake boards
7. Pastry brush
8. Turntable (for TV)
9. Non-slip rubber mat
10. Baking paper
11. DIY board
12. Pencils (2B)
13. Scraper

Decorating equipment

1. Wire
2. Alphabet cutters
3. Small rolling pin
4.+10. Broad and fine paintbrushes
5. Serrated dough wheel
6. Stitching tool
7. Balling tool
8. Frilling tool
9. Cotton wool
11. Tape measure
12. Plastic paint palette
13. Toothpicks
14. Ruler
15. Small rolling pin
16. Baking paper
17. Wooden skewers
18. Dowel
19. Piping tips and coupler
20. Piping bag
21. Flower cutter
22. Dropper
23. Star cutters
24. Aquarium tubing
25. Non-slip rubber mat
26. Pasta machine
27. Circle cutters

Glossary

Many items listed here are available from specialist cake-decorating suppliers. Some of the more everyday bits can be bought at the supermarket or cookware shops.

Acetate film is often described as plastic film or sheeting. This general-purpose plastic is an industry standard in graphic arts, packaging, printing and for overlays.

Aquarium tubing can be found in hardware stores or aquarium shops. This plastic tubing is inexpensive, comes in different diameters and has many different uses.

Balling tool This long plastic stick has a ball at either end. Use it to make round indentations and smooth curves in modelling or to shape flower petals.

Cachous or dragrees are round, edible sugar balls coated with silver or gold which are used for decorative purposes.

Cake boards are usually made from silver or gold masonite and are available from cake-decorating supply shops.

Set-up cake boards are the same size as the cake (for example, 22 cm/9 in round cake on a 22 cm/ 9 in round board) and they operate as a guide for ganaching and a way to easily handle the cake and not stain the display board.

The display cake board or 'final' board is the larger board the cake is placed on as part of its display; the display board is 10–15 cm (4–6 in) larger than the cake.

Cake dowels are long thin solid cylindrical plastic or wooden pillars, pointed at one end.

They are pushed into cakes to support pillars for holding tiered cakes. They are also useful for moulding and modelling. If they are to be inserted into the cake we recommend covering the dowel with food-safe tape.

Cornflour is used in cake decorating for dusting the work surface when rolling out icing. It must be used sparingly, as it can dry the icing out, but it is finer to use than icing sugar.

Couverture is a natural, sweet chocolate containing no added fats other than natural cocoa butter. It is used for dipping, moulding, coating and similar purposes.

Cutters are available in different sizes and shapes and often come in sets, in plastic or stainless steel.

Decorating alcohol has 5 per cent rose essence and is used for painting and removing icing stains. Vodka can be used as a substitute.

DIY cake board is a waxed cardboard template used as a substitute set-up board when decorating an unusual shape. For example, the Paint tube cake (page 172) requires you to make your own wax DIY board from the templates provided (see pages 186-9).

Edible glitter is available in an array of colours and is usually applied with water or piping gel.

Edible glue is also known as sugar glue. It is used to glue together dry pieces of icing such as securing dried modelling icing figurines to a dried cake. If both or one of the pieces were still soft, they could be stuck with just water or egg white, so often edible glue is not necessary.

Flexi-scraper is a Planet Cake invention. We use either unused X-ray film, which can be hard to get, or a thin plastic such as acetate, computer film or the plastic used for bendy display folders (the ones with the plastic sleeves inside). Cut the plastic to a rectangle a little larger than the palm of you hand, round the edges using scissors, and disinfect the plastic.

Florist tape can be twisted on its own to create an effect, but it can also be used to cover wires or dowels before inserting into the cake. Some are coated with a green paper.

Food colour Paste colouring is the most concentrated of food colours. Mix this paste directly into your fondant icing to colour it or mix it with alcohol to paint with. Liquid colouring is similar but less intense.

Frilling tool This tool is part of a set called 'modelling tools'. It's used to frill soft surfaces such as sugar paste, modelling paste, flower paste or marzipan.

Ganache is a mixture of chocolate and cream. It can be made with dark, milk or white chocolate and is used as a filling or icing for cakes.

Glaze is a product or mixture that gives a shiny appearance to cakes or decorations.

Glycerine is a colourless, odourless, syrupy liquid made from fats and oils and used to retain moisture and add sweetness to foods. Stir into icing to restore consistency or use to soften fondant or royal icing. It can also be used to soften dried icing colours.

Marzipan or almond paste is made from ground blanched almonds and icing sugar. It is used as a very thin layer on fruit cakes before they are covered with royal icing or sugar paste. Marzipan can also be used for making flowers and fruit.

Non-slip rubber mats are perfect for placing under your turntable or cake to prevent slipping. A mat is also great underneath the cake when placing it in a cake box for transport.

Paintbrushes Fine paintbrushes can be used for painting, brushing crumbs or icing sugar out of tricky corners, as well as applying powdered or liquid colours. Broad brushes are useful for cleaning debris off the cake board.

Palette knife The cranked palette knife is usually a plastic-handled knife with a bend (crank) in it, and is used to ganache cakes and cupcakes. The palette knife is a flat, metal palette knife used to smooth ganache, and can also be handy to transfer the cake from a temp board to the display board. Both types come in large and small sizes.

Parchment bag is a disposable decorating bag formed from a parchment paper triangle.

Pasta machine is also called a pasta maker. It is used for making home-made pasta and is useful to roll out icing as it provides a consistent thickness and rolls the icing perfectly.

Piping gel is a clear sticky gel that becomes fluid when warmed. It can be coloured for piping on dry sugar paste or royal icing. It maintains a shiny, wet look when set. Also known as piping jelly.

Piping tips and coupler These are specially shaped, open-end tips used to form icing decorations. The size and shape of the opening on a piping tip determines the type of decorations the tip will produce. Sometimes called decorating tubes or decorating tips. The coupler sits between the piping bag and piping tip. You can screw the piping tip onto the coupler and easily change between different sizes and shapes without changing the piping bag.

Powders and dusts are available in petal, pearl, sparkle and lustre finishes. Some decorators mix the powder with decorating alcohol and apply the colour directly. The lustre and pearl powders create a luminous effect to sugar flowers.

Rolled fondant icing Also called RTR (ready-to-roll), plastic icing, sugar paste and fondant is a dough-like icing that is rolled out, draped over the cake and then smoothed down. It is used to cover cakes and cupcakes. The basic ingredient of fondant is icing sugar with the addition of gelatine, corn syrup (glucose) and glycerine to provide a malleable sweet paste. Fondant gives the cake a beautiful, porcelain-like surface that can be painted, piped, quilted, cut out or stamped. Fondant comes in white or ivory and can be tinted to any colour of the rainbow. It is also used to model and cut three–dimensional shapes for decoration, such as ribbons, bows and cut-outs. Good-quality fondant is costly but worth buying.

Rolling pins A small rolling pin is ideal for small projects and rolling out small pieces of icing. You can buy a fancy one from a cake-decorating supplier, but the most prized small rolling pins at Planet Cake are those found in children's baking sets!

A large rolling pin is a long, smooth cylindrical roller mainly used to roll out pastry. A variety of types are available: without handles, with integral handles, or Planet Cake's favourite, with handles that are attached to a central rod in the roller. Rolling pins are usually made from wood but can also be made from marble or silicon. Choose a rolling pin you are comfortable with.

Royal icing is a mixture of egg white or albumen and icing sugar. It can be spread over cakes and boards and sets very hard. It is also used for piping. You can buy instant royal icing mixes where you just have to add water, or you can make your own using the recipe on page 33.

Scraper Best made of stainless steel, a side scraper is a flat piece of metal or plastic with a straight side that is used for scraping the excess ganache off the side of a cake when you are preparing and filling it. Metal scrapers can be sourced from cake-decorating suppliers and the internet. If you don't have a scraper you can use a metal ruler. Plastic scrapers are also fine to use.

Smoothers are also called 'paddles'. These rectangular, flat plastic paddles with handles are used for pressing the air bubbles out of fondant icing and rubbing it to a smooth shiny finish. For covering cakes you always need at least two smoothers.

Stitching tool, more properly known as a tracing wheel, is an instrument with serrated teeth on a wheel attached to a handle. A stitching tool is used in sewing to transfer markings from patterns onto fabric, but this tool also makes a perfect stitching effect in RTR icing. There are two basic types of tracing wheels available, one with a serrated edge and one with a smooth edge. You need to buy the serrated edged tracing wheel, which are available from haberdashers.

Syrup, sugar syrup or soaking syrup is a mixture made from equal amounts of boiled water and jam (recipe page 32). The syrup is brushed over the cut surfaces of cakes to prevent them drying out before icing. Syrup can be flavoured with alcohol such as Cointreau (orange liqueur).

Turntable is a useful tool for when you are coating cakes with royal icing or rolled icing as it allows you to approach the cake from all sides. You can just buy a turntable from a cake-decorating store but at Planet Cake we actually like to use the type that you would put under a TV set.

Tylose powder can be mixed into rolled fondant, marzipan or royal icing and forms a strong modelling paste that dries hard. Tylose powder can also be mixed with a small amount of water to make thick and strong edible glue.

Wire is available from cake-decorating stores. It comes in different thicknesses called gauges, and sometimes it is covered with paper. Use no. 22 gauge for the Exploding star cake (page 122).

Cake recipes

The wonderful thing about these cakes is that they actually taste great. Your cakes are going to taste as magnificent as they look.

Vanilla cupcakes

Makes 12 cupcakes

175 g (6 oz/¾ cup) unsalted butter, softened
160 g (5¾ oz/¾ cup) caster (superfine) sugar
1 teaspoon natural vanilla extract
1 teaspoon grated lemon zest
1 tablespoon Madeira (optional)
2 eggs
160 g (5¾ oz) self-raising flour
100 g (3½ oz) plain (all-purpose) flour
200 ml (7 fl oz) milk

1. Preheat the oven to 180ºC (350ºF/Gas 4). Line a 12-hole cupcake tray with paper cases.

2. Beat the butter, sugar, vanilla, lemon zest and a pinch of salt with electric beaters until pale and fluffy. Add the Madeira and beat until well combined. Add the eggs one at a time, beating well after each addition.

3. Sift the flours together. Using a wooden spoon, fold the flour and milk alternately into the creamed mixture.

4. Spoon into the paper cases and bake for 20–25 minutes or until a skewer comes out clean when poked into the middle of the cake.

5. Leave in the tray for 5 minutes before turning out onto a wire rack to cool.

Storage: Keep in an airtight container in the fridge for up to two days, or freeze for up to 1 month.

Chocolate mud cake

Makes one 22 cm (9 in) round cake
or one 20 cm (8 in) square cake

220 g (7¾ oz) butter
220 g (7¾ oz) dark chocolate,
    chopped
25 g (1 oz/½ cup) coffee granules
125 g (4½ oz) self-raising flour
125 g (4½ oz) plain (all-purpose)
    flour
50 g (1½ oz/⅓ cup) unsweetened
    cocoa powder
½ teaspoon bicarbonate of soda
480 g (1 lb 1 oz/1¾ cups) caster
    (superfine) sugar
4 eggs, lightly beaten
7 teaspoons vegetable oil
100 ml (3½ fl oz) buttermilk

1. Preheat the oven to 160°C (315°F/Gas 2–3). Grease the tin and line the base and sides with a collar that extends 2 cm (¾ in) above the top of the tin.

2. Put the butter, chocolate and coffee in a saucepan with 160 ml (5½ fl oz/⅔ cup) water and stir over low heat until melted, then remove from the heat.

3. Sift the flours, cocoa and bicarbonate of soda into a large bowl. Stir in the sugar and make a well in the centre. Add the combined egg, oil and buttermilk and the chocolate mixture, stirring with a large spoon until completely combined.

4. Pour the mixture into the tin and bake for 1 hour 40 minutes or until a skewer poked into the centre of the cake comes out clean, though it may be a little sticky. Leave the cake in the tin until cold.

Storage: Keep in an airtight container in the fridge for up to 3 weeks, or freeze for up to 2 months.

Carrot cake

Makes one 22 cm (9 in) round cake
or one 20 cm (8 in) square cake

170 g (5½ oz) self-raising flour
170 g (5½ oz) plain (all-purpose)
    flour
2 teaspoons ground cinnamon
1 teaspoon ground ginger
½ teaspoon ground nutmeg
1 teaspoon bicarbonate of soda
200 ml (7 fl oz) vegetable oil
225 g (7 oz/1 cup) soft brown sugar
4 eggs, lightly beaten
125 ml (4½ fl oz/¼ cup) golden syrup
500 g (1 lb 2 oz/3¼ cups) grated
    carrots
60 g (2 oz/½ cup) chopped pecans
    or walnuts

1. Preheat the oven to 170ºC (325ºF/Gas 3). Grease the tin and line the base and sides with a collar of baking paper that extends 2 cm (¾ in) above the top of the tin. Sift together the flours, spices and bicarbonate of soda into a large bowl and make a well in the centre. Whisk together the oil, sugar, egg and golden syrup. Gradually pour into the well, stirring until combined. Stir in the carrots and chopped nuts.

2. Spoon the mixture into the tin and smooth the surface. Bake in the oven for 1 hour 40 minutes or until a skewer poked into the middle of the cake comes out clean.

3. Leave the cake to cool in the tin for at least 15 minutes before turning onto a wire rack to cool completely.

Storage: Keep in an airtight container in the fridge for up to 1 week, or freeze for up to 2 months.

White chocolate mud cake

Makes one 22 cm (9 in) round cake
or one 20 cm (8 in) square cake

300 g (10½ oz) unsalted butter,
  chopped
300 g (10½ oz) white couverture
  chocolate, chopped
300 g (10½ oz) plain (all-purpose)
  flour
150 g (5½ oz) self-raising flour
400 g (14 oz/1¾ cups) caster
  (superfine) sugar
3 eggs, lightly beaten
1½ teaspoons natural vanilla
  extract

1. Preheat the oven to 180°C (350°F/Gas 4). Grease the tin and line the base and sides with a collar of baking paper that extends 2 cm (¾ in) above the top of the tin. Put the butter and 270 ml (9½ fl oz) water in a saucepan over medium heat and stir until the butter has melted. Turn off the heat, then add the chocolate and stir until it has melted and is well combined.

2. Sift the flours together into a bowl. Add the sugar, a pinch of salt and make a well in the centre.

3. Pour the chocolate mixture, egg and vanilla into the well then stir with a wooden spoon until well combined.

4. Pour into the cake tin. Bake for 1 hour 40 minutes or until the cake is golden brown and a skewer comes out clean when poked into the middle of the cake. Cover with foil halfway through if the cake is browning too quickly.

5. Leave to cool completely in the tin on a wire rack.

Storage: Keep in an airtight container in the fridge for up to 1 week, or freeze for up to 1 month.

Coconut cake

Makes one 22 cm (9 in) round cake
or one 20 cm (8 in) square cake

220 g (7¾ oz) butter, softened
325 g (11½ oz/1¾ cups) lightly
   packed brown sugar
1 teaspoon natural coconut extract
3 eggs, lightly beaten
130 g (4¾ oz/1⅓ cups) desiccated
   coconut
360 g (12¾ oz) self-raising flour
360 ml (12 fl oz) buttermilk

1. Preheat the oven to 180ºC (350ºF/Gas 4). Grease the tin and line the base
and sides with a collar of baking paper that extends 2 cm (¾ in) above the
top of the tin.

2. Beat the butter, sugar and coconut extract until light and fluffy. Add the
eggs one at a time, beating well after each one. Fold in the combined coconut
and sifted flour alternately with spoonfuls of buttermilk.

3. Spoon the mixture into the tin and smooth the surface. Bake for
1 hour 10 minutes until golden brown and a skewer poked into the middle of
the cake comes out clean.

4. Leave the cake in the tin for at least 5 minutes before turning out onto a
wire rack to cool.

Storage: Keep in an airtight container in the fridge for 1 week, or freeze for
up to 2 months.

Flourless orange and almond cake (dairy/gluten-free)

Makes one 22 cm (9 in) round cake
or one 20 cm (8 in) square cake

2–3 oranges (with unwaxed,
   unblemished skin as the whole
   fruit is used)
8 eggs
420 g (15 oz/1¾ cups) caster
   (superfine) sugar
1 teaspoon baking powder
420 g (15 oz/4¼ cups) ground
   almonds

1. Scrub the oranges well and leave them whole. Put them in a large saucepan with enough water to cover them. Put a small plate on top of the oranges to keep them submerged. Bring to the boil, then reduce the heat and leave to simmer gently for 1 hour until the oranges are very soft.

2. Grease the tin and line the base and sides with a collar of baking paper that extends 2 cm (¾ in) above the top of the tin.

3. Drain the oranges well, then put back in the saucepan and leave until cool enough to handle. Cut each orange into quarters, remove the pips, then purée in a blender or food processor.

4. Beat the eggs, sugar, baking powder and a pinch of salt until pale and creamy. Beat in the almonds and 420 g (15 oz) of the orange purée. Leave for 20 minutes and preheat the oven to 180°C (350°F/Gas 4).

5. Pour into the tin and bake for 1 hour 30 minutes until golden brown and a skewer poked into the centre comes out clean. Cool completely in the tin.

Storage: Keep in an airtight container in the fridge for up to 1 week, or freeze for up to 2 months.

Icing recipes

All the cakes in this book are first brushed with a little syrup, perfectly coated with chocolate ganache and then covered with a layer of rolled fondant icing. You'll find all these basic icing recipes in this chapter.

Ganache

The ideal chocolate for making ganache is a couverture variety with a cocoa content of 53–63%. In cold weather you might have to add a touch more cream or reduce the chocolate a little bit so that your ganache isn't too hard. If you can't find couverture chocolate, try dark chocolate from the baking section of the supermarket.

These recipes make approximately 1.8 kg (4 lb) of ganache, which is enough to cover each cake in this book (with a little leftover in case of mishaps).

White ganache
1.3 kg (3 lb) white chocolate, finely chopped
450 ml (16 fl oz) pure cream

Dark ganache
1.2 kg (2 lb 10 oz) dark chocolate, finely chopped
600 ml (21 fl oz) pure cream

1. To make either white or dark ganache, put the chocolate pieces in a large bowl.

2. Put the cream in a saucepan and bring to boiling point. Pour the cream over the chopped chocolate and mix with a hand whisk until the ganache is smooth. (Do not use an electric whisk, as you will create too many air bubbles in the ganache.)

3. Allow to cool completely and then leave to set overnight.

Microwave method

1. Put the chocolate and cream in a microwave-proof bowl and heat for 1–2 minutes on high then remove and stir. Repeat heating and then stirring until the ganache is smooth.

2. Remove the bowl from the microwave, cover with plastic wrap and leave for 5 minutes. Shake the bowl a little bit so all the chocolate sinks to the bottom.

3. Mix with a hand whisk until smooth.

4. Allow to cool completely and then leave to set overnight.

Facts about ganache

What is the difference between white and dark ganache?
The white chocolate ganache is sweeter and goes well with the coconut and carrot cake.
White chocolate ganache is less stable than dark chocolate ganache, so in hot weather or when you are making intricate three-dimensional cakes, it is easier to use dark chocolate ganache.

What type of cream do you use to make ganache?
I use pure cream ('single' or 'pouring' cream) for making ganache (never 'thickened' cream, which has gelatine added to it). Use a cream with a low fat content, which does not thicken when beaten.

How long does ganache keep?
You can keep ganache in the fridge usually for a week. However, always check the use-by date of your cream when you buy it and make sure it has at least one week's shelf life.

How do you store ganache?
The ganache recipe (page 31) makes enough to cover one cake, with a bit leftover in case anything goes wrong. But as I make so many cakes, I like to make a big batch of ganache and then decant it into smaller containers to be frozen. If you are planning on using the ganache during the next few days, keep it in the fridge and let it come back to room temperature before using.

How do you reheat your ganache?
Ganache that's taken straight from the fridge will be too hard to spread over the cake. Keep the ganache in smaller containers and heat as much as you need in the microwave in short bursts of 10–20 seconds. Stir after each burst, and make sure not to 'cook' your ganache or it will burn and curdle. If you don't have a microwave put the ganache in a saucepan and heat over low heat, stirring, making sure not to burn the ganache.

Syrup

100 g (3½ oz/⅓ cup) apricot jam
2 teaspoons orange liqueur
  (optional)

1. Whisk the jam with 100 ml (3½ fl oz) boiling water until smooth.

2. Remove any lumps and stir in the orange liqueur, if using.

Rolled fondant icing

I don't make my own fondant icing as I find the commercial varieties easier and more reliable to use. But if you do need a recipe, this one is courtesy of my friend Greg Cleary — a great cake decorator.

15 g (½ oz) gelatine
125 ml (4 fl oz/½ cup) liquid
   glucose
25 ml (5 teaspoons) glycerine
1 kg (2 lb 4 oz) pure icing sugar
2 drops flavour extract (optional)

1. Sprinkle the gelatine over 3 tablespoons water in a small bowl. Leave until the gelatine is spongy.

2. Place the bowl over a saucepan of hot water and stir until the gelatine has dissolved. Add the glucose and glycerine and stir until melted. Strain through a sieve.

3. Sift the icing sugar into a large bowl, make a well in the centre and pour in the gelatine mixture. Mix until it becomes too difficult to stir with a spoon. Tip the mixture out onto a bench, add the flavouring, if using, and knead with dry hands into a smooth and pliable dough.

4. Wrap the icing in plastic wrap and store in an airtight container in a cool place (but do not refrigerate).

5. Knead again before using, adding more sifted icing sugar as necessary.

Royal icing

Makes about 250 g (9 oz)

250–300 g (9–10½ oz) pure icing
   sugar, sifted
2–4 drops acetic acid
1 egg white

1. Beat 250 g (9 oz) icing sugar, the acetic acid and the egg white with electric beaters on medium–high speed for 4 minutes for 'soft peak' or over 5 minutes for 'firm peak' (or beat for 20 minutes by hand). Add extra sugar if the icing is still too soft after that time.

2. 'Soft peak' royal icing is used for coating cakes and piping with tubes. When lifted from the bowl with a spatula, the peak will stand up but droop over slightly at the tip.

3. Store the royal icing in an airtight container in a cool place but not in the fridge. It will keep for several days.

Note: Achieving the right consistency for royal icing can be difficult, so you may prefer to buy an instant royal icing mix where you just have to add water.

Techniques

The most important technique you'll learn in this chapter is the Planet Cake 'secret' for perfectly decorated cakes: using ganache as the base for a thin layer of RTR (ready-to-roll) icing.

Ganaching

Chocolate ganache (a melted mixture of chocolate and cream) will not only make your cake taste better and keep it moist, but will also give you a perfect surface for icing. At Planet Cake we use ganache as a sort of edible 'putty' to fill in all the crevices and holes in the cake and create an even surface to cover with rolled fondant icing.

Once the ganache has set hard and is perfectly smooth, it presents a firm and perfect surface for covering with thin icing (rather than the thick unpalatable icing that some decorators use to hide imperfections in the cake).

Follow the recipe for making ganache (page 31) and allow it to set overnight. If the ganache is too hard when you are ready to use it, heat it in short bursts in the microwave until it reaches the consistency of smooth peanut butter. If you don't have a microwave put the ganache in a pan and heat over low heat, stirring, making sure not to burn the ganache.

Alternatively, you could use a layer of buttercream under your fondant icing but it will not set as firm as ganache and so not give you the same perfect finish.

Ganaching cupcakes

Let the cupcakes cool completely after baking, but do ganache them on the same day to prevent them drying out.

1. Syrup (optional)
Cupcakes dry out very quickly. One way to prevent this is to treat them with syrup. With a fork or a skewer make some holes in the top of the cupcakes and then brush fairly liberally with syrup (page 32).

2. Even out the surfaces
If your cupcakes have spilled over their paper cases or risen unevenly, cut off the tops so that they are all even. It is very difficult to ice a high-domed cupcake.

3. Spread with ganache
Using a palette knife, spread a small dessertspoonful of ganache across the top of each cupcake.

Be very careful not to smear ganache onto the paper cases, particularly if you are using dark chocolate ganache.

4. Hot-knife
By the time you have ganached your last cupcake your first cupcakes should be set and ready to 'hot-knife'. This is the way we get such a smooth finish on our ganache. To achieve a perfect result you need a jug of boiling water and a long knife. Leave the knife to stand in the hot water for a few seconds, then glide it over the surface of the ganache using even pressure. When you ganache larger cakes you hold the knife at both ends, but cupcakes are a much more manageable place to start. Let the cupcakes sit until the ganache has set hard (preferably overnight) before you start decorating them.

Ganaching a round cake

1. Slice your cake horizontally into three even layers

Trim the dome from the top of the cake to get a flat surface. Put the cake on a turntable and place one hand on top of the cake (never keep your hand on the side as the knife could slip). Hold a long serrated knife in the other hand, making sure to keep the knife level.

Mark the cutting lines on the cake by scoring the side; each layer should be about 2.5 cm (1 in) thick. Rotate the cake and cut towards the centre with a sawing action, gradually cutting deeper. Continue turning and cutting deeper every round, making sure to keep the knife at the same horizontal level.

Repeat this one more time to cut another layer.

Tip: If your cake is cracked or uneven on the top, swap the middle layer with the top layer so that you can hide it inside the cake.

2. Brush with syrup

Place the three layers of cake on your work surface and brush each fairly liberally with syrup (page 32).

3. Fill the cake with ganache

Use a palette knife to spread some ganache on a cake board the same size as the cake; eg, a 20 cm (8 in) cake would be placed on a 20 cm (8 in) board. We refer to this board as the set-up or DIY board.

Apply ganache to each layer of the cake to about 1 cm (½ in) thick and sandwich the layers together.

Tip: Having a set-up or DIY board is very important when ganaching as it allows you to make a big mess and, most importantly, serves as a guide for measuring the filling. Cakes shrink during the baking process and

by placing the cake on the same size cake board you can see how much ganache to apply to bring the cake back to the correct size.

4. Apply ganache to the side

With a palette knife, apply ganache all around the side of the cake out to the edge of the set-up or DIY board. Do not put ganache on the top of the cake at this point.

5. Scrape off the excess ganache

Using the turntable, put one hand on the top of the cake and run the plastic scraper slowly around the side of the cake. Make sure to hold the scraper straight on the edge of the board and continue turning until your cake has a perfectly vertical edge and all the gaps are filled.

Tip: Your goal is to fill the side of the cake until it meets the rim of the set-up or DIY board. This may take some time and will require more ganache than you envisage. Make sure you have a perfect right angle — if the filling bulges out there will be a lump on your cake. Alternatively, if there is not enough ganache and the side is not flat you will have ridges.

6. Apply ganache to the top

Use a small palette knife to smear the excess ganache over the edge of the cake and onto the top, then level the top. Use more ganache on the top if necessary. Let set (preferably overnight) or freeze for a maximum of 10 minutes.

7. Hot-knife

To achieve a perfect result you will need a jug of boiling water and a long knife to run over the cake to make sure the edge is perfect. Take a large palette knife or the back of a bread knife and leave it to stand in

the hot water for a few seconds. Hold the knife at both ends and glide it over the surface of the cake, making sure to apply even pressure along the whole length of the knife. If the ganache is uneven, apply more to level the cake.

Run the plastic scraper once more around the side of the cake. Let the cake set again and, when it is hard, use a hot knife to cut the overhang off the top edge. Clean your board and leave the cake until the ganache has set hard (preferably overnight) before you cover it.

Ganaching a square cake

Follow the same guidelines as for the round cake until step 4.

The same method applies to rectangular cakes.

1. Ganache and smooth

Apply the ganache thickly to the sides (about 2 cm/¾ in) with a palette knife to build up the cake. Scrape off the excess with a scraper and apply more ganache until you have very sharp edges. Smooth the ganache, then let set until it is firm to the touch (1–2 hours). Apply ganache on the top, smooth and let set (preferably overnight).

2. Hot-knife

Hot-knife the ganache starting at one side and then glide over the surface (making sure to apply even pressure along the length of the knife) scraping off any excess ganache. Run the plastic scraper once more along the sides and take special care to keep the corners sharp.

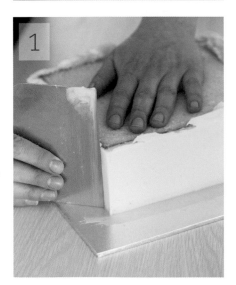

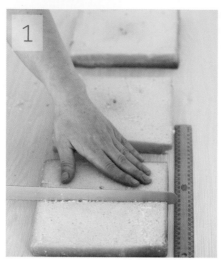

Cutting and ganaching a rectangular cake

All the recipes for shaped cakes call for rectangular cakes. This is how to shape a 20 cm (8 in) square cake into a 30 x 20 cm (12 x 8 in) rectangular cake and then ganache it.

1. Slice the cake into layers
Place a 20 cm (8 in) square cake on a clean work surface or turntable and cut the dome from the top of the cake to get a levelled surface. Place one hand on top of the cake (never keep your hand on the side as the knife could slip). Hold a long serrated knife in the other hand, making sure to keep the knife level, then slice the cake twice horizontally to make three even layers.

Spread out the three layers and brush each one with syrup (page 32). Cut one layer in half to 20 x 10 cm (8 x 4 in).

2. Make and fill a rectangle
Take one of the half layers and sandwich it on one normal layer with ganache. Put the other normal and half layer on top and sandwich them together with ganache. Trim the sides and place the cake on a set-up or DIY board of 30 x 20 cm (12 x 8 in).

3. Apply ganache to the sides and top
Put the cake on a turntable. Apply a little bit of ganache on the cake to seal the crumbs, then apply more ganache around the sides with a palette knife until you get a rectangle of 20 x 30 cm (12 x 8 in). Slowly run the scraper along the sides, making sure you are holding it straight on the board and at a right angle. Use a small palette knife to smooth the excess ganache from the sides up over the edges and onto the top. Even the top, using more ganache if necessary (see ganaching a square cake, page 39).

Let set (preferably overnight). To speed up the process you can freeze the cake for a maximum of 10 minutes until the ganache is firm to the touch.

4. Hot-knife
To achieve a perfect result you will need a jug of boiling water and a long knife to run over the cake to make sure the edges are perfect. Take a large palette knife or the back of a bread knife and leave it to stand in the water for a few seconds. Hold the knife at both ends and

glide it over the surface of the cake, making sure to apply even pressure along the length of the knife. If the ganache is uneven, apply more to level the cake.

5. Perfecting the edges
Run your plastic scraper along the sides of the cake. Let the cake set hard for several hours or preferably overnight. When it is set hard, use a sharp knife to cut the overhang off the top edge.

Cutting and ganaching a shaped cake

After you have shaped your square cake into a rectangle, and before you ganache the sides, you need to make a template from cardboard that will also act as a DIY board (page 62).

1. Build up the cake
Place the template/DIY board on top of your cake and, using a sharp knife held at a right angle, cut around it. If the cake is not large enough, use the off-cuts to build up your shape, using ganache as edible glue.

2. Cut into shape
Cut around the template/DIY board at a right angle to make the shape.

3. Place cake on DIY board
Put the shaped cake on the DIY board. Roughly ganache the finished shape and let it set. Hot-knife and then let it set again.

Cutting and ganaching a three-dimensional cake

These cakes always need to be cut into two or three even layers and filled with ganache to achieve a certain height and stability. Put the cake onto a set-up or DIY board. Let the ganache set so the cake will be firm and easier to work with.

1. Build up the cake
To create the required shape, use the cake off-cuts and stick them together with ganache. Press them firmly into shape and stick the pressed pieces onto the cake.

Use your hands to mould and press the cake pieces together until you have the required shape.

2. Cut into shape
Using a serrated knife and with a sawing action, cut off excess cake and trim into shape. Let the cake rest for 1–2 hours. Ganache the whole cake, smooth and let set. Ganache and let set again, then hot-knife.

Using ready-to-roll (RTR) icing

RTR icing dries very quickly so you need to work fast to avoid it becoming cracked and difficult to use. Always work with small amounts of icing. Keep the icing you are not working with in a plastic bag or cover it with a plastic sheet to prevent it drying out.

The weather will affect your RTR icing: humidity will make the icing sticky and very cold weather will make it as hard as rock. I sometimes wait a day if it is bad fondant weather!

Cool your hands in cold water before you knead icing and use only a light sprinkling of cornflour. When kneading your icing on a bench, it is a good idea to lean over the icing so you can use your body weight to help you knead. Never cover a cake that you have taken straight from the fridge as it will sweat underneath the icing. To achieve a professional finish let your cake come to room temperature first.

Never use icing that is too dry or that has been over-kneaded, or you will find the corners will crack very easily. When you are making dark colours that require a lot of food colour such as red, black, brown or purple, colour the icing a day in advance so it has time to relax and rest.

Once you have covered your cake, do not refrigerate as the icing will sweat and become soggy. Store your decorated cake in a cool dry place (up to 20°C/68°F).

Any leftover RTR icing is best stored in a sealed plastic bag or airtight container. Please follow the manufacturer's instructions on how to store your particular brand of icing. I store my icing at room temperature.

Covering cupcakes

1. Roll the icing and cut out circles
Roll out the icing to 3 mm (⅛ in) thick with a pasta machine or rolling pin. Cut out circles with a round cutter in the closest size to your cupcakes. Keep the icing discs covered with a plastic sheet to prevent them drying out.

2. Smooth the icing
Brush each cupcake with syrup (page 32) and stick the icing disc on top. Push the icing into place until it sits perfectly on the surface of the cupcake, and then use a flexi-scraper to smooth the icing.

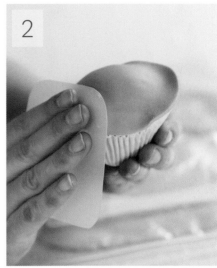

Covering a round cake

Make sure your cake is smoothly ganached and allowed to set before you cover it with icing. The more perfectly the cake is ganached, the better the final result will be.

1. Prepare the cake

Wipe your work surface clean and make sure it is dry. Measure the cake (side and top surface). Brush the cake all over with a little syrup (page 32); this helps the fondant stick to the cake.

Stick your cake on a set-up board or on its display board with a bit of royal icing and place the board on a non-slip mat so that is does not slip while you are working on it.

2. Flatten and roll the icing

Make sure your icing is smooth. Flatten your ball of icing first with the palm of your hand to about 4 cm (1½ in) thickness before rolling it with the rolling pin (this makes it easier to roll). Knead the icing to a pliable dough using a sprinkle of cornflour if it sticks.

Lightly dust your work surface with cornflour. Roll the icing, starting from the centre rolling about six times in one direction.

Turn the icing and repeat the process. If your work surface gets sticky use a bit more cornflour but never use cornflour on top of the icing! The turning of the icing will ensure that the icing will always be a square, which will make covering a round or square cake much easier.

Keep on rolling and turning until your icing is about 3 mm (⅛ in) thick; the icing needs to be larger than the total cake measurement.

Note: Kneading icing is not like kneading dough. If you keep pummelling it, it will stick to the board and become unmanageable. Treat your icing a bit like play dough: keep folding it in until it is smooth and warm to use but doesn't stick.

3. Lift the icing over the cake

Pick up the icing by rolling it onto the rolling pin. Use a dry pastry brush to remove any excess cornflour (this is particularly important if you use dark-coloured icing).

Lift the rolling pin with the icing up and unroll it over the cake starting from the base of the cake.

4. Secure the edges

Quickly run your hand over the top surface to make sure there are no air bubbles. Secure the edges by running the palms of your hands along the top edge and side of the cake.

5. Smooth the icing

Press the icing gently on the side, working around the cake. Pull the icing away from the side of the cake before smoothing it down.

6. Use icing smoothers

Once the whole cake is covered, gently press the icing against the side and base of the cake using icing smoothers.

7. Trim the icing

Trim the icing around the base with a pizza wheel or a knife.

Tip: Do not trim your icing too close to the base of your cake as the icing shrinks and you could be left with a gap. If this does happen, adjust your design and place a roll around the base of the cake (page 62).

8. Use your smoothers

Run your smoothers along the side of the cake. I use two smoothers to do this job; the one in the left hand is running back and forth and the one in the right hand is pressed against the cake to make a sharp edge. Hold one smoother on the side of the cake and the other one on the top surface. Using the same amount of pressure, press them together and run along the side of the cake to give a sharp edge.

Glide your hand along the cake feeling for air bubbles. If there are any, poke a small pin into the bubble and gently release the air with your dry fingers (page 65).

Go over the cake with your smoother or flexi-scraper to buff and polish the icing.

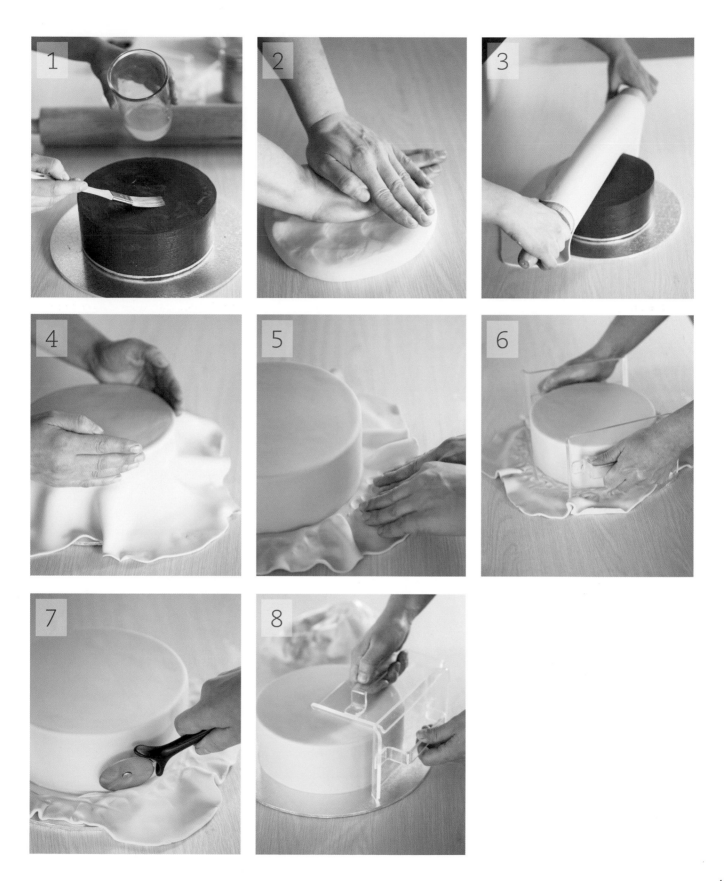

Covering a square cake

Follow the same guidelines as for the round cake until step 3 (page 44).

Once the cake is covered, quickly secure the surface by running your hands along the top, smoothing and pressing the icing.

1. Secure the corners
Secure the corners immediately by running your hands towards the corner and pressing the icing onto the cake.

2. Push the icing down
Push the icing right down the corners with your fingers by running up and down along the edges.

3. Pull and smooth the sides
Gently pull the icing away from the sides with one hand and smooth it down with the other hand. Then run your hands up again to avoid tears or cracks in the icing. Trim the icing all around the base using a small knife or pizza wheel.

4. Smooth the icing
Use two flexi-scrapers and run them towards each other at the corners to achieve a sharp edge.

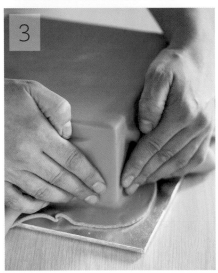
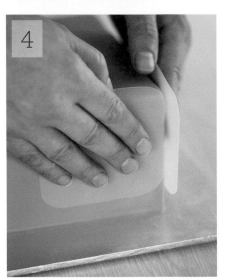
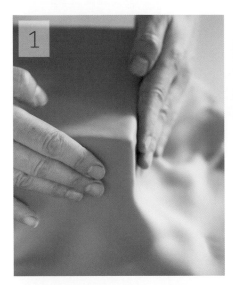
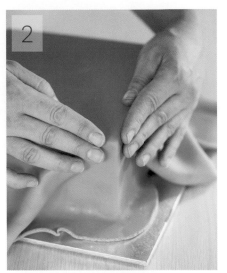

Covering shaped cakes

Covering a shaped cake will always be different depending on the design. Therefore feel your ganached cake with your hands, getting to know each crease and turn and also remove any crumbs or sharp edges, before you start icing your cake.

1. Secure the edges and smooth the icing
Secure the edges and all creases with your hands and fingers. Smooth the icing by gently pulling the icing away from the side before smoothing it down with your hand.

2. Trim the icing
Cut away the overhanging icing with scissors. Smooth the joining line with your fingers or a flexi-scraper. Trim the icing around the base with a small knife or pizza wheel.

3. Polish the icing
Using your flexi-scraper, buff and polish the icing against the shape of the cake, creating a more defined shape. Gently work the cake with your hands and flexi-scraper making sure you eliminate any air bubbles.

4. Secure edges
Cover the dome with icing. Secure the edge and smooth the icing with your hands.

5. Cut off excess icing
Mark a cutting line around the cake first, then cut off the excess icing with a small knife.

6. Apply icing sideways
Roll your icing onto a small rolling pin and unroll the icing around the cake, like unrolling a carpet.

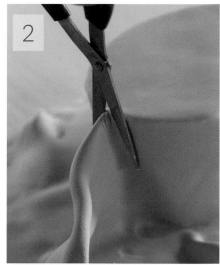

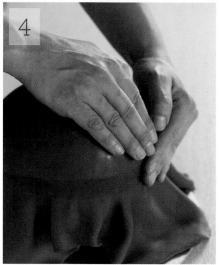

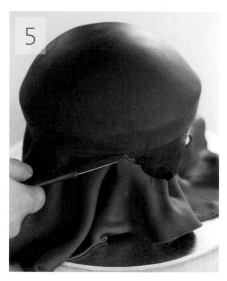

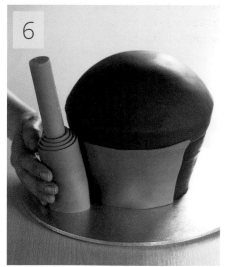

Covering a board with icing

There are two methods of covering a cake board: to cover the whole board, or just to cover the part that is visible around the cake. And it isn't necessary to cover your board at all — in fact many decorators don't. I cover my boards because I like the clean finish it gives (and I also personally don't like the look of silver or gold boards, which can undermine the effect of the cake).

Covering the whole board

1. Roll out the icing
Roll the icing to 3 mm (⅛ in) thick and at least the same size as the board. Place the icing on the board. If it is too small, keep on rolling it directly on the board until it covers the whole surface.

2. Make the icing stick
Dip a pastry brush in some water, lift the icing halfway up and brush the board. Lay the icing down and do the same to the other side.

3. Trim the icing
Use a flexi-scraper or an acrylic smoother and go over the surface to create a neat finish. Trim away most of the excess icing with scissors. Place the iced board on a turntable or halfway over the table and, using the acrylic smoother, hold it at a 45° angle and slide along the edge to cut the icing. This will give you a nice bevelled edge.

4. Place the cake on the board
Let the icing on the board dry, then stick the cake onto it with a dab of royal icing (page 33) to keep the cake on the set-up or DIY board.

Tip: If you choose to use this method to cover your board it is essential that your cake sits on a set-up or DIY board. For round and square cakes you can use ready-made boards as set-up boards. For shaped cakes you will need to make your own DIY board from waxed cardboard (page 62).

Covering a board around the cake

For round and square cakes

Prepare and cover the cake on the final display board (pages 44–46).

1. Roll the icing and use a cake board as a template

Roll the icing to about 3 mm (⅛ in) thick and at least the same size as as the final display board. Place a cake board in the exact same size as the cake or a little smaller in the centre of the rolled icing and cut it out using a small paring knife.

Tip: I always cut the template a bit smaller than the size of the cake, because when you lift the icing it will automatically stretch slightly.

2. Place the icing

Lift the icing carefully over the cake, and push and manipulate the icing to fit snugly around the cake.

3. Make the icing stick to the board

Trim some of the excess icing with scissors. Lift the icing up and brush a bit of water on the board.

4. Smooth the icing

Stick the icing down and with a flexi-scraper smooth it out. Use an acrylic smoother to cut the icing on a 45° angle to the board.

Tip: For a perfect finish, place a thin ribbon around the board. Place the board on a turntable and stick the ribbon around the edge by using glue. Make sure the ribbon joins at the back of your cake.

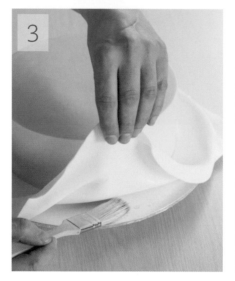

Covering a board around the cake

For shaped cakes

Prepare and cover the cake on the final display board (page 47).

1. Roll the icing and use a DIY template

Roll the icing to about 3 mm (⅛ in) thick and at least the same size as the final display board. Use the template of your cake and cut the icing around it. Use a clean paring knife to do this. It is particularly important for the shaped cakes to use a template. However, for rounds or squares we just use a cake board.

2. Place the icing

Cut a slit in the icing at the back to allow access for the cake. Like placing a horseshoe, place the icing on the board and around the cake making sure the slit is at the back.

3+4. Manipulate and trim the icing

To make sure the icing meets at the back for a perfect join, let the icing overlap a little. Then trim to make the edges of the icing meet perfectly. Push and manipulate the icing to fit snugly around the cake.

5. Make the icing stick

Lift the icing up and brush a bit of water on the board. Stick the icing down and with a flexi-scraper smooth it out.

6. Trim the icing

Use an acrylic smoother to cut the icing on a 45 degree angle to the board.

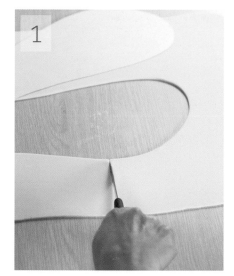

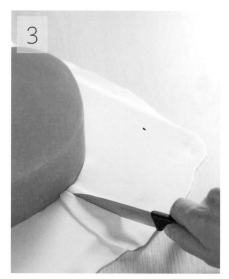

51

Techniques, tips and trouble-shooting

When you're starting off, making a bow or a tassel or even a perfect layer of thinly rolled icing can seem daunting. Follow these step-by-step instructions and you'll see how easy it all is. And, however experienced and wonderful a decorator you become, occasionally things will go wrong. That doesn't mean you have to start again — our trouble-shooting guide will show you how to deal with the common problems that occur.

Colouring icing

1. Measure the colour
Knead the icing to a pliable dough. Add only a tiny amount of food colour at a time.

2. Add the colour
Smear the colour onto the icing, then knead until it's evenly distributed. Wear gloves to prevent staining your hands.

3.+4. Check the colour
Cut through your icing to check if the colour is evenly blended. If there are still swirls of colour, keep kneading, and checking, until the colour is solid all the way through. Or, leave the colour as it is for a marbled effect in your icing.

Tip: When you want to colour your icing very strongly, making deep colours such as black, brown, red, purple or royal blue, it's better to use paste food colour. Since you need much more colour, a liquid colour would make the icing too sticky to work with. Even if you're using paste, colour your icing a day in advance as it will be exceptionally soft due to the large amount of colour pigment.

Fading: Some colours are more prone to fading than others. Pink shades are susceptible to fading out quickly when exposed to sunlight. Pink and mauve can be reduced to almost white, purples to blues, blues to grey, and black to purple or green. Avoid the problem by either covering your cake with a clean cloth or keeping it in a cake box.

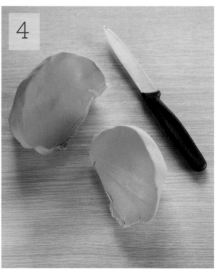

Using a pasta machine to roll icing

1. Roll out the icing first with a rolling pin

Work out which setting on your pasta machine will roll pasta (or icing) to 3 mm (⅛ in). This is the usual thickness we use for covering most cakes. Knead and roll out the icing first with a small rolling pin.

2. Run the icing through the pasta machine

Feed your piece of icing through the pasta machine, and keep feeding it through until it reaches a 3 mm (⅛ in) thickness, just as you would a piece of pasta.

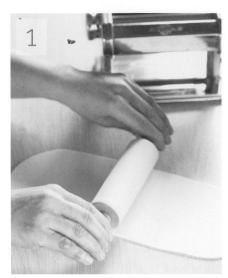

Glazing icing

For glazing icing you can either use jam diluted with boiling water (strain to remove any lumps), or olive oil cooking spray. Apply the glaze with a paintbrush as close as possible to the time you are serving the cake. There is also a professional product (you can buy this from cake supply shops) which is a clear gel for glazing tortes and fruits.

Sticking icing

Icing is made from sugar and so will 'stick' to itself with the addition of water alone. You can use syrup (page 32) instead of water, if you prefer. Paint a very faint line of water on the icing and stick the other icing piece onto it. Don't apply too much water or the icing will become soggy. To stick icing onto aquarium tubing or acetate, use piping gel.

Making a tassel

Method one

1. Roll the icing through the pasta machine

Roll the icing to 3 mm (⅛ in) thick in the pasta machine. Then use the spaghetti setting on the pasta machine and roll the icing through it to make thin lengths.

2. Fold the icing threads over to make a tassel

Fold your 'spaghetti' over and pinch together at the top. 'Tie' with a thin piece of icing rope. Finish the tassel with a twisted icing rope, made from two icing rolls twisted together to look like tassel cord.

Method two

1. Make a tassel with a knife

Shape a rectangular block of icing of about 1 cm (½ in) thick. Slice it thinly with a knife, pinching it at the top and creating a thin rope of icing near the top.

Piping with royal icing

Tip: The round piping tips used for royal icing come in an assortment of sizes no. 00 –12 and the numbers correspond with the size of the hole, no. 00 being the smallest.
No. 1 piping tip and smaller could be frustrating for new decorators, so it's better to start with a no. 2 tip or bigger and gradually work to fine piping. If you are only piping with royal icing and not with buttercream, you will only need a couple of round piping tips to start.

Making royal icing: You can make your royal icing from scratch (recipe page 33) or buy instant royal icing mix, which is a good substitute. Before piping with royal icing, it is essential to have it at the correct consistency: not too runny, and not too thick as it will keep blocking the piping tip.

Tip: Royal icing dries to a very hard consistency and it will begin setting as soon as it is made, so always keep it covered with plastic wrap.

Colour: If you wish to colour your royal icing, add food colour in very small quantities and mix the royal icing and colour together using a palette knife. You can do this on a board or plate. Don't make the colour too dark as it will darken when it dries.

Equipment: Disposable plastic and material icing bags are perfect for home decorating. If you have a material bag like the one pictured in our equipment chapter, you will need a coupler as well as a piping tip.

1. Fill the bag
Only fill the piping bag one-third full with royal icing and push the icing down towards the piping end of the bag. Give it a few squeezes to get rid of the air pockets. If you find it difficult to hold the bag and fill it at the same time, you can place the bag in a glass to hold it while you fill it.

2. Pipe
Practise some lines before you start piping on the cake. Fit the piping bag with a plain piping tip in the size you desire. Hold the bag correctly with two hands, one hand to guide and the other to squeeze the bag. Hold the piping bag at a 45° angle just above the work surface. Apply pressure and see the icing emerge from the tip. Secure the end of the icing thread to the surface, then pipe, allowing the thread to fall into position.

Tip: Start with simple designs and practise until you feel confident. To create board messages you need to learn a 'font'.

Tracing letters and applying edible glitter

1. Trace onto tracing paper
Trace your desired image or font onto baking paper using a 2B pencil. Fold the baking paper over and trace the back of the same image.

2. Place it on the cake
Place the template right side up on the cake and, by lightly shading your baking paper, transfer the image onto the cake.

3. Apply piping gel
Using a fine paintbrush apply piping gel to your traced image.

4. Dust with edible glitter
Dust the wet area with edible glitter and allow it to dry.

5. Brush away excess glitter
Dust away the excess glitter with a soft brush.

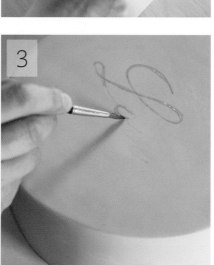

Making a bow

1. Roll the icing
Roll your icing to 3 mm (⅛ in) thick with a rolling pin or in a pasta machine. Cut two rectangles of 13 x 25 cm (5 x 10 in). Cover the icing you are not working on with a plastic sheet, so it doesn't dry out and crack. With a small paintbrush, lightly brush along the two short sides of the rectangle with water.

2. Pleat the icing
Pinch pleats on both short sides of the rectangle simultaneously.

3. Use cotton wool as filling
Put cotton wool in the centre of the rectangle. Remove when the icing has dried.

4. Fold the icing over
Fold one side over to bring both pleated sides together and gently press the ends together.

5. Sit the bow loop up
Lift the bow loop up (as it would sit on the cake) and fold one side underneath. You should now have half a bow. Place the folded side on a board and repeat the same process with the other icing rectangle.

6. Trim the ends
Trim the centre a little and push the bow loops together.

7. Make the bow knot
Roll out your leftover icing to 3 mm (⅛ in) thick. Cut a small rectangle of white icing to about 8 x 10 cm (3¼ x 4 in). Fold the short side into pleats to get the bow knot.

8. Assemble the bow
Place the bow knot over the ends of the bow loops, pinch the edges together. Trim at the back.

Making a zipper

1. Mark the icing

Roll out the icing to about 3 mm (⅛ in) thick and cut it into a rectangle to the length you require. Cut out two strips, one 6 mm (¼ in) wide and the other 2.5 cm (1 in) wide. Cover the icing with a plastic sheet to prevent it drying out. Run a serrated dough wheel along the centre of the thin strip to mark the zipper teeth. Use your ruler and stitching tool to mark a line on both edges of the wider strip. Stick the thinner strip of icing on top of the wider strip.

2. Paint the zipper

Mix decorating alcohol and edible gold dust and paint the zipper using a fine paintbrush.

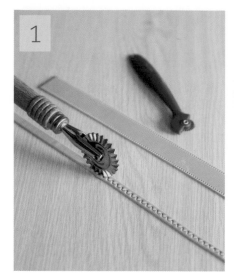

Covering acetate film

Acetate film is a flexible plastic used in stationery or computer laser printing. It is also a good 'frame' for creating cake decorations such as flip flop straps, as you can insert the film into the icing or cake and it will be invisible and light.

1. Brush the acetate with piping gel

Apply the piping gel with a brush onto your strip of acetate.

2. Place the icing on the acetate

Place a strip of icing on either side. Trim the excess and smooth down any fuzzy bits with a damp finger. You can either cover the film before or after it is inserted into the cake. If you are covering beforehand,

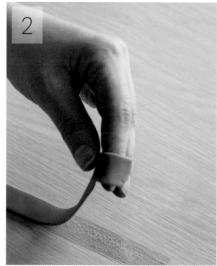

leave the area to be inserted into the cake without icing and cover any unsightly joins.

Note: Remember to advise those eating the cake that this decoration is inedible.

Making sand icing

1. Mix and colour the sand
Mix 150 g (5½ oz) royal icing and 70 g (2½ oz) raw sugar together. Add one drop of coral brown food colour at a time until you get a sand colour.

2. Apply with a palette knife
Apply the sand icing with a palette knife to your board or cake immediately as it will start drying quickly and become rock hard.

Making coals

Roll out a piece of dark grey icing to 5 mm (¼ in) thick. Place pieces of orange, red and black icing on the grey icing in a random pattern. Carefully roll over with a rolling pin to about 3 mm (⅛ in) thick.

Frilling

Roll a small piece of icing into a rectangle of 2 mm (¹⁄₁₆ in) thickness. Firmly roll the frilling tool back and forth using your other hand to catch the icing as it bunches. To create a long frill (required for the princess cake, page 104) do short strips of frilling and join them together on the cake with a dab of water.

Basic painting

Mix a small amount of food colour with decorating alcohol and paint a test piece of icing first. Work quickly, as the 'paint' dries almost instantly. Work with small quantities at a time.

Tip: The silver and gold dust can spread everywhere. To prevent this, cover unpainted areas on your cake with paper.

Making an icing roll

1. Roll the icing with your hands
Using your hands, roll the icing to the basic shape of a rope.

2. Roll even with a smoother
Using an icing smoother, roll the rope back and forth, pulling it slightly out to the sides to elongate it. If the icing begins to slip under the smoother and does not roll easily, use your paintbrush to paint a thin line of water right next to and parallel with the rope, then use the smoother to roll the icing across the water. This will make the icing a little bit stickier, which will help it 'catch' and roll easily underneath the smoother. Continue to roll and stretch the icing rope until it is the desired width and length.

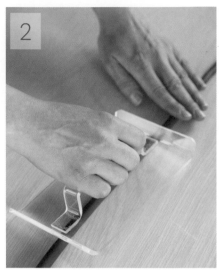

Marking a paper cupcake case

Make the indentations for the 'paper case' using a wooden dowel. You can also use a barbecue skewer or a chopstick.

Making a template and a DIY board

Enlarge and trace one of the templates from this book onto baking paper and cut out to create the DIY template. Place it on top of waxed cardboard and cut around it to create the DIY board. Put the DIY board under the cake so you can move it around more easily.

Mending torn icing

1. Gap in icing
Tearing is usually the result of smoothing and pulling your icing down too vigorously when covering.

2. Smooth the tear
While the icing is still soft, use your hands and a flexi-scraper and massage the icing up and around the tear so that the tear gap is closed and almost invisible. If you are still left with a hole, wait until the icing has dried (next day). Make a small ball of fresh icing in the same colour as your base and massage the fresh icing into the tear like putty. Smooth with a flexi-scraper and allow to dry.

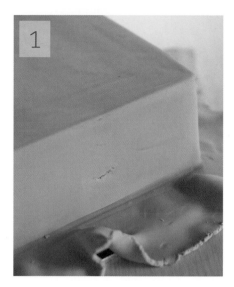

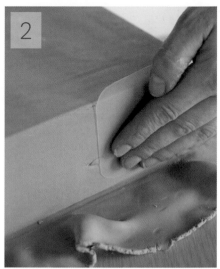

Covering up cracked icing

Cracks usually appear on corners or edges when the icing is too dry. A huge crack is impossible to fix, but you can cover it up with some decorations such as icing flowers so nobody will notice it.

Mending cracked icing

While your icing is still soft, use very warm hands and massage the icing inwards around the cracks, closing them and rendering them until almost invisible.

Cleaning stained icing

Cornflour stain

1. Apply decorating alcohol
Apply decorating alcohol with a soft paintbrush on the stain. The alcohol will absorb the cornflour.

2. Pat dry
Pat the spot dry with a soft tissue.

Chocolate stain

1. Wash with soapy water
Use a soft paintbrush and wash the stain lightly with a very small amount of warm soapy water.

2. Dust with cornflour
Rinse your brush and wash the soap away with clean water. Lightly dry with a tissue and then lightly dust with cornflour using a soft brush.

Humidity

Due to humidity, icing often becomes soft and sticky. To solve this, mix sifted icing sugar into the icing a little at a time and knead it through.

Icing too dry

If your icing is dry and cracking, apply a little water to it, using a brush, then knead it through. Alternatively, brush the icing with a small amount of glycerine (see glossary, page 17) and knead it through.

Icing too wet

Wet icing is usually the result of too much colour pigment. Therefore black, red and brown icing often become 'wet' and difficult to work with. To solve this, knead sifted icing sugar into your icing a little at a time until it becomes less sticky but is still pliable.

Air bubbles

Feel over your cake for air bubbles, then lightly prick any with a pin to let the air escape, then smooth over your icing with a flexi-scraper. Always try to eliminate air bubbles under your icing as they will get bigger and lift the icing.

Cupcakes

I have yet to discover anyone who doesn't love cupcakes, so what better (or easier) place to start? These make a great introduction to the equipment and techniques needed for decorating larger cakes, such as using ganache, and colouring and handling the icing.

All cupcake designs by Anna Maria Roche.

Bow cupcakes

Material
12 cupcakes
100 ml (3½ fl oz) syrup
250 g (9 oz) ganache
500 g (1 lb 2 oz) pink icing
(cupcakes)
500 g (1 lb 2 oz) black icing (bows)
Cornflour

Equipment
Skewers
Pastry brush
Cranked palette knife
Large and small rolling pins
Pasta machine
Plastic sheets
Set of circle cutters
Flexi-scraper
Cornflour
Small kitchen knife
Paintbrush

Syrup the cupcakes
Follow the instructions on how to syrup cupcakes (page 37).

Ganache the cupcakes
Follow the instructions on how to ganache cupcakes (page 37).

Cover the cupcakes
Knead the pink icing to a pliable dough and roll out to 3 mm (⅛ in) thick. Using a circle cutter in the same size as the cupcakes, cut out 12 circles and stick them onto the cupcakes (page 43).

Make the ribbon strip
Roll out 200 g (7 oz) of the black icing to 3 mm (⅛ in) thick (be careful not to get cornflour on top of the icing). Cut strips of 1 cm (½ in) wide and slightly longer than the width of the cupcake and cover with plastic to prevent drying. Mark a line of water across the centre of each cupcake and place the ribbon strip. Trim the ends with a sharp knife so the strip sits flush with the cupcake (step 1).

Make the bow loops
Roll out 300 g (10½ oz) of the black icing (be careful not to get any cornflour on top of the icing). Cut two 1 cm (½ in) wide strips, one strip about 10 cm (4 in) long and then a shorter strip. Fold the ends of the longer strip over to make bow loops, and stick in place with a dab of water. Cover the centre with the shorter strip, making a faux knot (steps 2+3) and attach to the ribbon strip with a dab of water (step 3).

Tip: Insert tissue paper in the loops and remove when the icing has dried.

Glaze (optional): Follow the instructions on how to glaze (page 54). Glaze the ribbon and bow.

1. Place a strip of black icing across the middle of each cupcake to make the ribbon and trim the ends. 2. Fold the ends of the longer strip over and glue in place with a dab of water. Cover the centre with the shorter strip to make a knot. 3. Attach the bow to the ribbon strip with a dab of water.

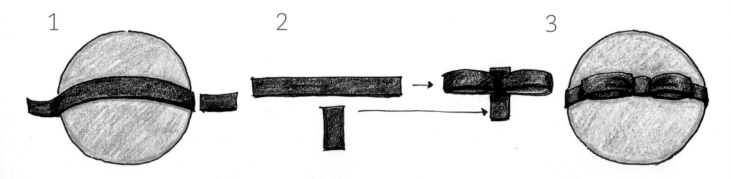

Dragonfly cupcakes

Material
12 cupcakes
100 ml (3½ fl oz) syrup
250 g (9 oz) ganache
500 g (1 lb 2 oz) purple icing
  (cupcakes)
250 g (9 oz) white icing (wings)
250 g (9 oz) deep purple icing
  (dragonfly)
Florist wire or mung bean noodles
Cornflour

Equipment
Skewers
Pastry brush
Cranked palette knife
Large and small rolling pins
Pasta machine
Set of circle cutters
Flexi-scraper
Plastic scraper
Paintbrush
Heart cutter
Small kitchen knife

1. Cover the cupcakes. 2. Cut the wings using a heart cutter and then cut them in half.
3. Apply the body of the dragonfly in a curved line. 4. Attach the wings and add the antennae.

Syrup the cupcakes
Follow the instructions on how to syrup cupcakes (page 37).

Ganache the cupcakes
Follow the instructions on how to ganache cupcakes (page 37).

Cover the cupcakes
Knead the purple icing to a pliable dough and roll out to 3 mm (⅛ in) thick. Using a circle cutter in the same size as the cupcakes, cut out 12 circles and stick them on the cupcakes (page 43).

Make the wings
Roll out the white icing in a pasta machine (page 54) or by hand and cut two hearts per cupcake with the heart cutter, then cut them in half (step 2).

Make the body
Use the deep purple icing to roll seven to eight balls per cupcake graduating in size from a baby pea to a large pea. Paint a curved line of water on the cupcake and stick the balls on the icing starting from the largest size (step 3). Attach the wings (step 4).

Make the antennae
Use two small pieces of mung bean noodles or thin wire per cupcake as antennae. Roll two tiny balls of white icing and stick them on the ends of the noodles.

Note: When making the cupcakes for children, use mung bean noodles for the antennae as they are edible.

71

These sweet little baby cupcakes make the perfect gift for a baby shower. If you don't know whether the baby's going to be a boy or a girl, just use a mix of pastel colours for the beanies and dummies. For a first birthday party, you could even pipe the baby's name onto the beanies.

Baby cupcakes with beanies and dummies

Material
12 cupcakes
100 ml (3½ fl oz) syrup
250 g (9 oz) ganache
500 g (1 lb 2 oz) skin-coloured icing (mix red, orange and brown/ cupcakes)
Red petal dust
Cornflour
50 g (1¾ oz) white icing (eyes)
50 g (1¾ oz) black icing (eyes)
200 g (7 oz) light blue icing (beanies)
250 g (9 oz) pink icing (dummies)
250 g (9 oz) yellow icing (quiffs)

Equipment
Skewers
Pastry brush
Cranked palette knife
Large and small rolling pins
Pasta machine
Plastic sheets
Set of circle cutters
Flexi-scraper
No. 2 piping tip
Paintbrushes
Frilling tool
Clear plastic drinking straw

Syrup the cupcakes
Follow the instructions on how to syrup cupcakes (page 37).

Ganache the cupcakes
Follow the instructions on how to ganache cupcakes (page 37).

Cover the cupcakes
Knead the skin-coloured icing to a pliable dough and roll to 3 mm (⅛ in) thick. Using a circle cutter in the same size as the cupcakes, cut out 12 circles and stick them on the cupcakes (page 43).

1

2

3

4

5

6

1. Use the frilling tool to make the indents for the eyes.

2. Use the circle cutter to cut out the beanies and then cut in half. Add the trim and pompom.

3. Attach the eyes.

4. Make the dummies.

5. Make the hair quiff and bow.

6. Attach the dummy, hair quiff and bow.

For rosy cheeks, mix red petal dust with cornflour (to dilute) and dust on the face with a dry paintbrush.

Make the nose and ears

Roll a small ball of skin-coloured icing for the nose and stick it in the centre of the face with a little water. With the frilling tool mark two holes for the eyes. Make two balls from skin-coloured icing for the ears and stick them on either side of the face, level with the nose. Press the frilling tool into each ball to give them an ear shape (step 1).

Make the mouth

While the icing is still soft, use the edge of a round cutter to indent the mouth on the babies that will not have a dummy (step 2).

Finish the eyes

Roll out tiny balls of white icing and stick them into the indents. Using tiny amount of black icing, roll out even smaller balls and stick them on top of the white balls (step 3).

Make the beanie

Roll out the light blue icing to 3 mm (⅛ in) thick. Cut out circles, using the same size circle cutter you used for the cupcake. Cut off one-third with the same cutter, then stick the beanies on the cupcakes. Roll a piece of the light blue icing into a small ball and stick it onto the beanie to make a pompom. Re-roll the light blue icing to 3 mm (⅛ in) thick, cut a thin strip and stick it on the beanie's rim. Trim and decorate (step 2).

Make the dummy

Roll out the blue icing to about 5 mm (¼ in) thick and cut out a circle of 2 cm (¾ in) with a piping tip. Make a roll of pink icing and cut it to a 5 mm (¼ in) cylinder. Stick the cylinder on the circle with a little water (step 4). Stick the dummies in the cupcakes without noses, with a little water (step 6).

Make the hair quiff and bow

For the quiff, roll a small amount of yellow icing into a cone, twist the cone and stick it to the head with a little water (steps 5+6).

For the bow, roll blue icing to 3 mm (⅛ in), and cut two strips, one three times longer than the other. Fold the long strip inwards to the centre for the bow loops. Fix the short strip on the centre for the bow knot. Stick the bow on the hair quiff with a little water (steps 5+6).

Honeybee cupcakes

Material
60 g (2¼ oz) white icing (wings)
12 cupcakes
100 ml (3½ fl oz) syrup
250 g (9 oz) ganache
500 g (1 lb 2 oz) chocolate brown
   icing (cupcakes)
250 g (9 oz) yellow icing (stripes)
50 g (1¾ oz) black icing (stinger)
20 g (¾ oz) white icing (eyes)
20 g (¾ oz) black icing (eyes)
Mung bean noodles
20 g (¾ oz) yellow icing (antennae)
Cornflour

Equipment
Skewer
Pastry brush
Cranked palette knife
Large and small rolling pins
Pasta machine
Set of circle cutters
Flexi-scraper
Small kitchen knife
Frilling tool
Paintbrushes
Heart cutter
Plastic drinking straw

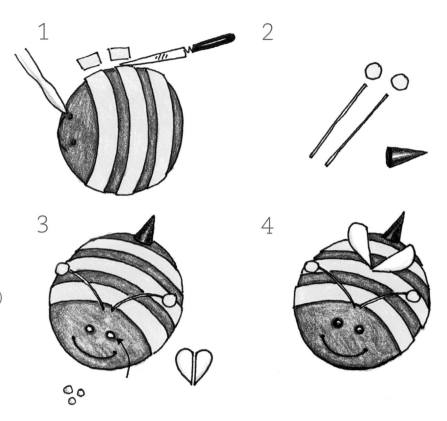

1. Trim the yellow stripes and make two indents for the eyeholes. 2. Make the antennae and the stinger. 3. Stick white dots of icing into the indents for the eyes and make the wings. Attach the antennae and stinger. 4. Finish the eyes and apply the wings.

Make the wings
Knead a small amount of white icing and roll out to 3 mm (⅛ in) thick. Cut out hearts with a heart cutter, then cut in half and trim the point. Gently curl the wings over a pen. Let dry for at least a day.

Syrup the cupcakes
Follow the instructions on how to syrup cupcakes (page 37).

Ganache the cupcakes
Follow the instructions on how to ganache cupcakes (page 37).

Cover the cupcakes
Knead the chocolate brown icing to a pliable dough and roll out to 3 mm (⅛ in) thick. Using a circle cutter the same size as the cupcakes, cut out 12 circles and stick them on the cupcakes (page 43).

Make the stripes
Roll out the yellow icing to 3 mm (⅛ in) and cut three to four 10 x 1 cm (4 x ½ in) strips for each cupcake. Stick the strips on the cupcake with a dab of water. Trim the edges with a sharp knife (step 1).

Make the antennae and stinger
Use two 1.5 cm (⅝ in) long mung bean noodles for the antennas. Roll two tiny balls of yellow icing and stick them on the ends of the noodles (step 2+3). Shape a small cone from the black icing and stick it on with a little water (step 2+3).

Make the face
Use a frilling tool to indent two holes for the eyes (step 1). Cut a drinking straw in half to mark the mouth. Roll out tiny balls of white icing and stick them into the indents. Using tiny amount of black icing, roll out even smaller balls and stick them on top of the white balls (steps 3+4). Poke in the antennae.

Place the wings
Pipe a small amount of white royal icing on the centre of the bee and stick on the dried wings.

Green monster cupcakes

Material
12 cupcakes
100 ml (3½ fl oz) syrup
250 g (9 oz) ganache
500 g (1 lb 2 oz) black icing
   (cupcakes)
300 g (10½ oz) green icing (face)
250 g (9 oz) white icing (eyes and
   teeth)
50 g (1¾ oz) orange icing (eyes)
100 g (3½ oz) red icing (lips)
Cornflour

Equipment
Skewer
Pastry brush
Cranked palette knife
Large and small rolling pins
Pasta machine
Circle cutter
Flexi-scraper
Small kitchen knife
Frilling tool
Paintbrushes

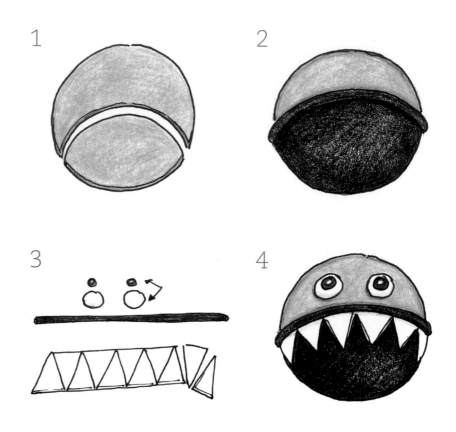

1. Use the circle cutter to cut the green icing and then cut again to create the face.
2. Apply the face to the top half of the cupcake and then add the red lips. 3. Cut the white icing to make the teeth and eyes, roll the red icing for the lips and the orange icing for the pupils. 4. Apply the teeth and the eyes.

Syrup the cupcakes
Follow the instructions on how to syrup cupcakes (page 37).

Ganache the cupcakes
Follow the instructions on how to ganache cupcakes (page 37).

Cover the cupcakes
Knead the black icing to a pliable dough and roll out to 3 mm (⅛ in) thick. Using a circle cutter in the same size as the cupcakes, cut out 12 circles and stick them on the cupcakes (page 43).

Make the head
Roll out the green icing to 3 mm (⅛ in) thick and using a circle cutter cut a circle the same size as the cupcake. Use the same cutter and cut a half section out (step 1). Stick the remaining crescent moon shape on the cupcake with a little water; align with the icing at the rim.

Make the lips
Roll a strip of red icing (the width of the cupcake) and thin it out towards the ends. Stick the roll on the joining line between the black and the green icing. Trim at the sides (step 2).

Make the teeth
Roll one-third of the white icing to 3 mm (⅛ in) thick. Cut a strip of 2 x 10 cm (¾ x 4 in) with a clean knife. Cut a zigzag for the teeth (step 3). Stick five to six teeth straight below the red icing.

Make the eyes
Roll pieces of the remaining white icing into pea-size balls and stick two on each monster's head. Using a frilling tool, make a hole in the centre of each ball. Roll very small balls of the orange icing and stick those into the holes of the white icing with a little water (steps 3+4).

Ladybird cupcakes

Material
12 cupcakes
100 ml (3½ fl oz) syrup
250 g (9 oz) ganache
500 g (1 lb 2 oz) black icing
    (cupcakes and dots)
500 g (1 lb 2 oz) red icing (wings)
Mung bean noodles
20 g (1¾ oz) white icing (eyes)
20 g (1¾ oz) black icing (eyes)
Cornflour

Equipment
Skewer
Pastry brush
Cranked palette knife
Large and small rolling pins
Pasta machine
Set of circle cutters
Flexi-scraper
Small kitchen knife
Frilling tool
Plastic drinking straw
Paintbrushes

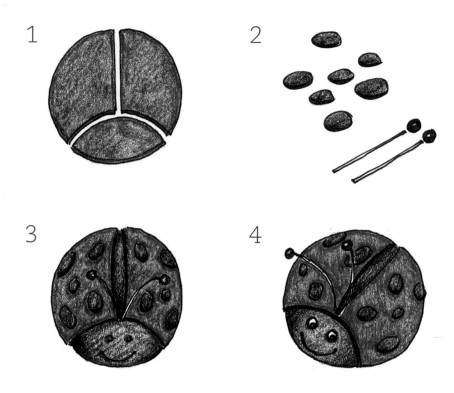

1. Use a round cutter to cut a disc of red icing for the wing cases. 2. Make the black spots and antennae. 3. Fix the spots to the wing cases with a dab of water and add the antennae. 4. Finish the eyes.

Syrup the cupcakes
Follow the instructions on how to syrup cupcakes (page 37).

Ganache the cupcakes
Follow the instructions on how to ganache cupcakes (page 37).

Cover the cupcakes
Knead 450 g (1 lb) of the black icing to a pliable dough and roll out to 3 mm (⅛ in) thick. Using a circle cutter in the same size as the cupcakes, cut out 12 circles and stick them on the cupcakes (page 43).

Make the wing cases
Set aside a small quantity of red icing for the antennae, then roll out the red icing to 3 mm (⅛ in) thick. Cut out discs using a round cutter the same size as the cupcake. Use the round cutter to cut out one-quarter of the discs. Cut the remaining portion of the icing disc in half. Stick the two wing cases on the cupcake with a little water, moving them slightly apart (step 1).

Knead the remaining black icing and roll into baby pea-sized balls (step 2). Flatten the balls between your fingers and stick them on the wing cases (step 3).

Make the antennae
Roll two tiny balls of red or black icing and stick them on top of two short sticks of mung bean noodles. Poke the noodles into the cupcakes, just behind where the eyes will be (steps 2+3).

Make the face
With the frilling tool indent two holes for the eyes. Use a drinking straw cut in half to mark the mouth. Roll out tiny balls of white icing and stick them into the indents. Using tiny amount of black icing, roll out even smaller balls and stick them on top of the white balls to finish the eyes (steps 3+4).

Pirate cupcakes

Material
12 cupcakes
100 ml (3½ fl oz) syrup
250 g (9 oz) ganache
500 g (1 lb 2 oz) skin-coloured icing
  (mix red, orange and brown/
  cupcakes)
150 g (5½ oz) red icing (bandana)
20 g (1¾ oz) white icing (eye)
20 g (1¾ oz) black icing (eye)
40 g (1½ oz) black icing (eyepatch)
Gold cachous
Red and brown food colour (scar)
Decorating alcohol
Cornflour

Equipment
Skewer
Pastry brush
Cranked palette knife
Large and small rolling pins
Pasta machine
Set of circle cutter
Flexi-scraper
Small kitchen knife
Frilling tool
Paintbrushes

Syrup the cupcakes
Follow the instructions on how to syrup cupcakes (page 37).

Ganache the cupcakes
Follow the instructions on how to ganache cupcakes (page 37).

Cover the cupcakes
Knead 450 g (1 lb) of skin-coloured icing to a pliable dough and roll out to 3 mm (⅛ in) thick. Using a circle cutter in the same size as the cupcakes, cut out 12 circles and stick them on the cupcakes (page 43).

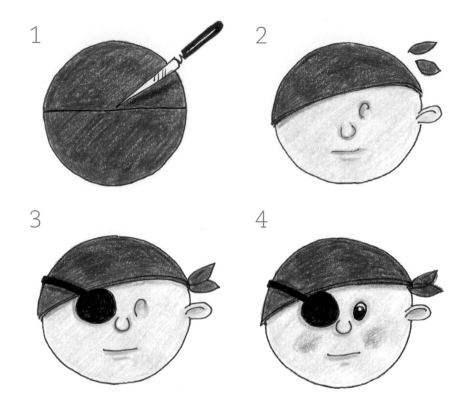

1. Cut a circle of the red icing in half. 2. Complete the bandana and mark the face. Add the ear. 3. Attach the eyepatch and strap. 4. Finish the eye with a dot of black icing.

Make the bandana
Roll the red icing to 3 mm (⅛ in) thick and cut out a disc with the same circle cutter. Cut the disc in half and stick on the cupcake at an angle with a little water (steps 1+2). Cut out two small leaves and pinch them slightly together at one end. Stick them on the side of the bandana with a little water (step 2).

Make the face and scar
Roll a small ball of skin-coloured icing for the nose and stick it onto the face with a little water. With the frilling tool indent one hole for the eye. Roll out tiny balls of white icing and stick them into the indents. Using a tiny amount of black icing, roll out even smaller balls and stick them on top of the white balls.

Use a paring knife to make the pirate's mouth. Make a ball from skin-coloured icing for the ear and stick it near the knot under the bandana. Press the frilling tool into the ball to make an ear shape (step 2). Stick one cachou into the ear as an earring and paint a scar (brown food colour mixed with decorating alcohol) onto the face.

Make the eyepatch
Roll a bit of black icing to the size of a small pea, flatten it between your fingers and straighten it on one side. Stick it just below the bandana in the line with the eye. Roll a very fine sausage out of the remaining black icing and stick on one side of the bandana across it to create the eyepatch strap (step 3+4).

Naughty kids cupcakes

Material

12 cupcakes
100 ml (3½ fl oz) syrup
250 g (9 oz) ganache
500 g (1 lb 2 oz) skin-coloured icing
   (mix red, orange and brown/
   cupcakes)
Red petal dust
Cornflour
200 g (7 oz) brown icing (hair)
200 g (7 oz) black icing (hair)
200 g (7 oz) orange icing (hair)
200 g (7 oz) yellow icing (hair)
20 g (1¾ oz) white icing (eyes)
20 g (1¾ oz) black icing (eyes)

Equipment

Skewer
Pastry brush
Cranked palette knife
Large and small rolling pins
Pasta machine
Set of circle cutters
Flexi-scraper
Small kitchen knife
Frilling tool
Paintbrushes

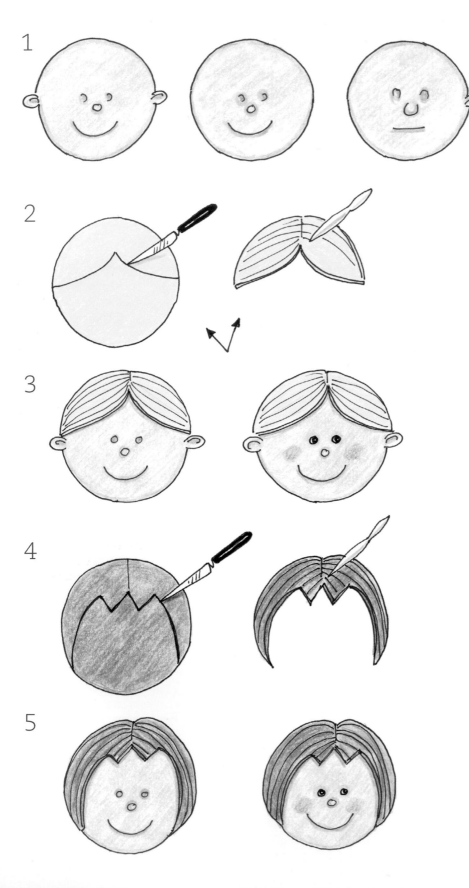

1. Use skin-coloured icing for the face, add the nose and ears and use the frilling tool to indent the eyes and freckles.

2. Cut the disc into the boy's hair shape and style with the frilling tool.

3. Apply the boy's hair with a dab of water and finish the eyes.

4. Cut the disc into the girl's hair shape and style with the frilling tool.

5. Apply the girl's hair and finish the eyes.

1

2

3

4

5

You can change the colour of the hair and skin icing if you want them to resemble those you know.

Syrup the cupcakes
Follow the instructions on how to syrup cupcakes (page 37).

Ganache the cupcakes
Follow the instructions on how to ganache cupcakes (page 37).

Cover the cupcakes
Knead 450 g (1 lb) of the skin-coloured icing to a pliable dough and roll out to 3 mm (⅛ in) thick. Using a circle cutter in the same size as the cupcakes, cut out 12 circles and stick them on the cupcakes (page 43).

Make the face
Roll a small ball of the remaining skin-coloured icing for the nose and stick it in the centre of the face with a little water. With the frilling tool, mark two holes for the eyes and use the edge of a round cutter or a knife to indent the mouth.

Make two balls from skin-coloured icing for the ears and stick them on either side of the boys' faces, level with the nose. Press the frilling tool into each ball to give them an ear shape (step 1). To give them a freckled look, mark small dots around the nose with the frilling tool.

Tip: Create the rosy cheeks by mixing red petal dust with cornflour (to dilute) and dusting on with a dry paintbrush.

Make the hair
Roll brown, black, orange and yellow icing to 3 mm (⅛ in) thick. Using the same round cutter as for the skin, cut out a disc. Cut the disc into the boy's or girl's hair shape with a small knife. Use the frilling tool to add lines for a natural look (steps 2+4). Stick the hair on the cupcake with a little water (steps 3+5).

Make the eyes
Roll out tiny balls of white icing and stick them into the eye indents. Roll out even smaller balls of black icing and stick them on top of the white balls to finish the eye. Cut a drinking straw in half lengthways and poke it into the face to mark the eyebrows.

Crying babies cupcakes

Material
12 cupcakes
100 ml (3½ fl oz) syrup
250 g (9 oz) ganache
500 g (1 lb 2 oz) skin-coloured icing
(mix red, orange and brown/
cupcakes)
200 g (7 oz) black icing (mouth)
150 g (5½ oz) red icing (tongue)
60 g (2¼ oz) white icing (teeth)
Black food colour
Decorating alcohol
60 g (2¼ oz) yellow icing (quiffs)
Red petal dust
Cornflour

Equipment
Skewer
Pastry brush
Cranked palette knife
Large and small rolling pins
Pasta machine
Set of circle cutters
Flexi-scraper
Small kitchen knife
Frilling tool
Paintbrushes

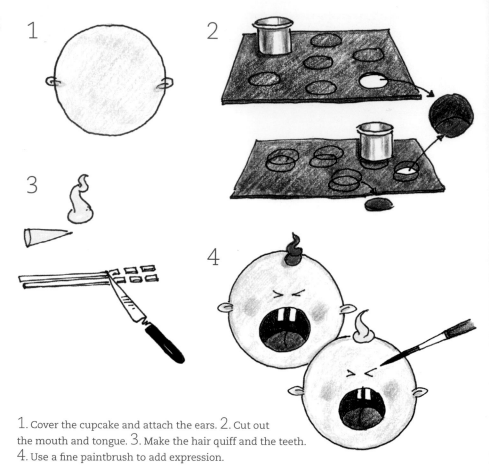

1. Cover the cupcake and attach the ears. 2. Cut out the mouth and tongue. 3. Make the hair quiff and the teeth. 4. Use a fine paintbrush to add expression.

Syrup the cupcakes
Follow the instructions on how to syrup cupcakes (page 37).

Ganache the cupcakes
Follow the instructions on how to ganache cupcakes (page 37).

Cover the cupcakes
Knead 450 g (1 lb) of skin-coloured icing to a pliable dough and roll to 3 mm (⅛ in) thick. Using a circle cutter in the same size as the cupcakes, cut out 12 circles and stick them on the cupcakes (page 43).

Make the ears
Make two balls of the remaining skin-coloured icing and stick them on either side of the face. Press the frilling tool into each ball to create the ear shape (step 1).

Make the mouth
Roll out the black, red and white icing to each 3 mm (⅛ in) thick. Using a small circle cutter, cut a black circle for the mouth and stick it on the face with a little water. Then, using an even smaller circle cutter, cut a red circle and cut the circle again for the tongue. Stick the tongue on the mouth (step 2).

With a sharp knife cut the white icing into long thin strips and then into rectangles for the teeth (step 3) and stick two onto the mouth.

With a paintbrush paint a line on the tongue with black food colour mixed with decorating alcohol (step 4).

Make the eyes
Use the paintbrush to paint two thin lines like meeting chopsticks on the face with black food colour mixed with decorating alcohol (step 4).

Make the hair quiff
Roll the yellow icing (or any colour you wish) into a cone then twist the cone between your fingers and stick it onto the head with a little water (step 3+4).

Tip: For rosy cheeks, mix red petal dust with cornflour, dust on the faces with a dry paintbrush.

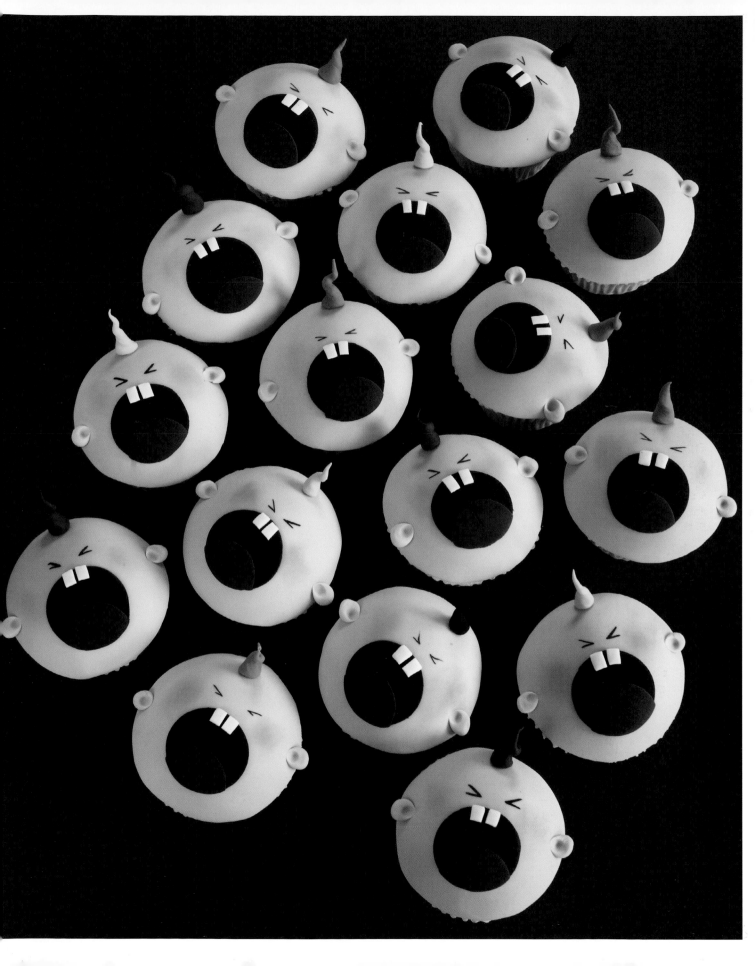

Round cakes

The round cake is the simplest basic shape for beginner decorators — there are no tricky angles or corners to deal with. You'll be amazed to see what you can produce with the skills you've already mastered. (Of course, when you bring out your cake, don't tell anyone else how easy it was!)

For little boys who love their toy cars, or big boys who love their toys, this cake is a perennial winner. But what an easy place to start. This will introduce you to using a template.

Racing car cake

Materials

22 cm (9 in) round cake
Hot glue or craft glue
7 lengths no. 22 gauge wire
100 ml (3½ fl oz) syrup
1.5 kg (3 lb 5 oz) ganache
1.5 kg (3 lb 5 oz) blue icing (cake)
250 g (9 oz) grey icing (border)
400 g (14 oz) black icing (wheels and extras)
30 g (1 oz) orange icing (hubcap)
60 g (1 oz) red icing (cars)
60 g (1 oz) green icing (cars)
60 g (1 oz) yellow icing (cars)
60 g (1 oz) orange icing (cars)
200 g (7 oz) white icing (clouds and extras)
700 g (1 lb 9 oz) white icing (board)
Glaze
Piping gel

Equipment

Ganaching tools (page 14)
22 cm (9 in) round board (set-up)
35 cm (14 in) round board (display)
Large and small rolling pins
Smoothers
Flexi-scraper
Frilling tool
Pastry brush
Wire cutter (secateurs)
Set of circle cutters
Pizza wheel
Baking paper (car templates)
2B pencil
No. 2 piping tip
Pasta machine
Ruler
Paintbrushes
Plastic sheet
Balling tool (optional)

Make the flags on wires

Use a photocopier to make 14 copies of the racing flag (page 189). Cut out and glue the flags to the top of the wires, using craft glue. Stick one copy on each side. Leave on a flat surface to dry (step 5, page 94).

Prepare the cake

Follow the instructions on how to prepare and ganache a round cake (page 38). Allow to set.

Cover the cake

Knead the blue icing to a pliable dough. Using a large rolling pin, roll out the icing to about 3 mm (⅛ in) thick. Follow the instructions on how to cover a round cake (page 44).

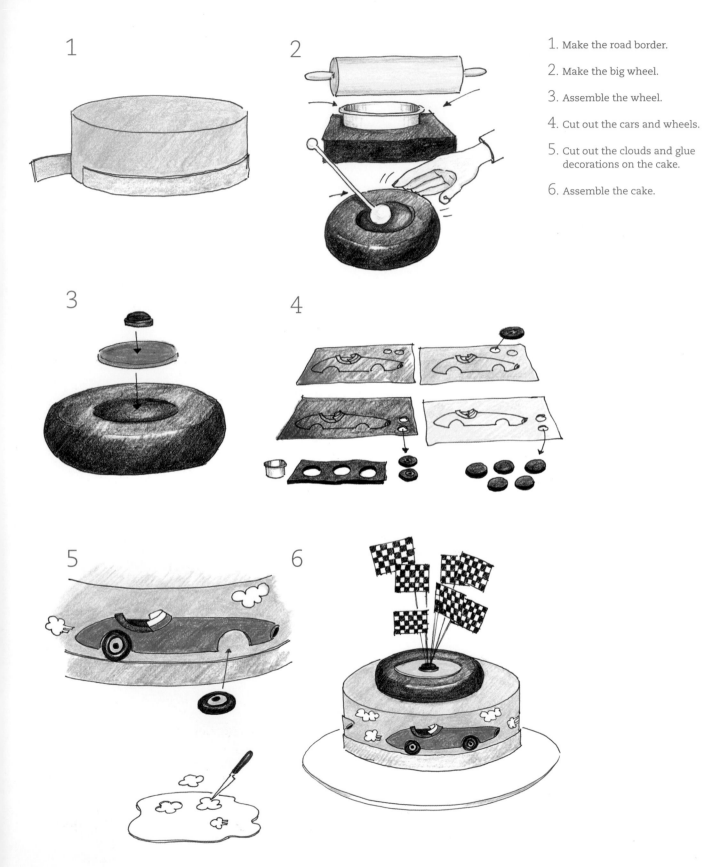

1. Make the road border.

2. Make the big wheel.

3. Assemble the wheel.

4. Cut out the cars and wheels.

5. Cut out the clouds and glue decorations on the cake.

6. Assemble the cake.

You can use the clouds to camouflage any rips or cracks in the icing.

Make the road border

Roll out the grey icing to 3 mm (⅛ in) thick. Use a ruler and pizza wheel to cut a strip 40 cm (16 in) long and 2.5 cm (1 in) wide. Cover with plastic. Lightly brush a line of water around the bottom of the cake to stick the strip on. Roll the strip onto a small rolling pin and unroll it around the cake. Overlap the icing at the join and cut it with a sharp knife so that it meets perfectly. This is now the back of the cake (step 1).

Make the big wheel

Roll out 50 g (1¾ oz) of the black icing to 2 cm (¾ in) thick. Use a 10 cm (4 in) circle cutter to cut out the wheel. Mould and round the edges of the wheel with your fingers. Use a balling tool to indent the centre of the wheel (step 2).

Roll out the orange icing to 3 mm (⅛ in) thick and use a large circle cutter to cut out the hubcap. Roll out a small amount of black icing and use a piping tip to cut the centre of the hubcap. Mould into a dome.

Assemble the wheel

Place the hubcap and the centre on the wheel and adjust the indent to fit. Fix with water and allow to dry.

Make the cars and clouds

Enlarge the car template (page 189), trace on baking paper and cut it out. Roll out the four car colours to 3 mm (⅛ in) thick and cut out the cars (step 4). Use a piping tip to cut out eight mini hubcaps, two from each colour. Cover the icing with plastic.

Roll out the black icing to 5 mm (¼ in) thick and use two small circle cutters (one slightly smaller than the other) to cut out eight tyres. Round the tyres slightly with your finger. Assemble the wheels, the smaller ones being the front wheels, using a dab of water. Add a small ball of flattened black icing in the centre of the hubcaps (step 4).

Make the template for the clouds and exhaust smoke. Roll out the white icing to 3 mm (⅛ in) thick and cut them out. Stick the clouds on with a dab of water (step 5).

Assemble the cars

Stick the cars on with water and polish with the flexi-scraper. Use your car template to create car trims from the white and black icings. A simple trim is a small, flattened roll of icing. Stick them on the cake with a little water. Do not polish with the flexi-scraper. Stick the car wheels on with water.

Attach the wheel

Stick the big wheel on the top of the cake with royal icing. Let dry.

Cover the display board

Knead the white icing to a pliable dough and roll out to 3 mm (⅛ in) thick. Follow the instructions on how to cover a board (page 48).

Glaze (optional)

Follow the instructions on how to glaze (page 54). Glaze the wheels.

Place the flags

Trim the wires to create height variation and poke the flags into the centre of the big wheel (step 6).

The decorations here are very crisp, clean and effective — but also incredibly achievable for the beginner. The basic technique for cutting out the skull and crossbones can easily be applied to just about any design of your choice.

Pirate cake

Materials
22 cm (9 in) round cake
100 ml (3½ fl oz) syrup
1.5 kg (3 lb 5 oz) ganache
1.2 kg (2 lb 10 oz) blue icing
600 g (1 lb 5 oz) white icing (board)
200 g (7 oz) white icing (skull and
   crossbones)
50 g (1¾ oz) red icing (bandana)
100 g (3½ oz) grey icing (cutlasses)
20 g (¾ oz) black icing (handles)
50 g (1¾ oz) yellow icing (stars)
200 g (7 oz) red icing (seam)
Silver cachous
Decorating alcohol
Royal icing
Edible silver or gold dust

Equipment
Ganaching tools (page 14)
22 cm (9 in) round board (set-up)
35 cm (14 in) round board (display)
Large and small rolling pins
Cranked palette knife
Smoothers
Serrated knife
Small sharp kitchen knife
Flexi-scraper
Pastry brush
Frilling tool (or toothpick)
Paintbrush
Piping bag
No. 2 piping tip
Pasta machine
Baking paper
2B pencil
Plastic sheets
Star cutters (various sizes)

Prepare the cake
Follow the instructions on how to prepare and ganache a round cake (page 38).

Cover the cake
Knead the blue icing to a pliable dough. Roll to 3 mm (⅛ in) and follow the instructions on how to cover a round cake (page 44).

Cover the display board
Knead the white icing to a pliable consistency. Follow the instructions on how to cover a board (page 48).

Decorate the side with cachous
Straight after covering the cake and while the icing is still soft, use the frilling tool to make small indents in the side of the cake in a random pattern. Press one cachou into each indent.

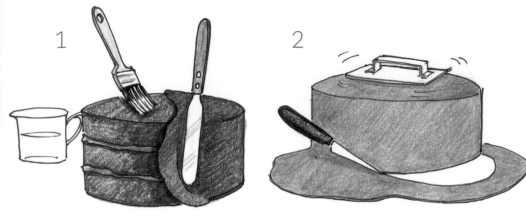

1. Apply the syrup and ganache.

2. Cover and smooth the cake.

3. Cover the board.

4. Cut out the skull and crossbones using the template.

5. Cut out the cutlasses and stars for the side decorations.

6. Apply the decorations.

For a three-dimensional effect, place tissue paper underneath the flaps so they are slightly raised and remove when the icing has dried.

Use the flexi-scraper to smooth the side of the cake so the cachous are even with the icing.

Tip: Avoid marking the icing with your fingerprints by using a frilling tool. If the cachous are not sticking to the icing, attach them with a little royal icing.

Create the template cut-outs
For the skull and crossbones, enlarge the template with a photocopier (page 187), trace it on baking paper and cut it out. Roll out the 200 g (7 oz) of white icing in a pasta machine or with a rolling pin to about 3 mm (⅛ in) thick. Lightly dust a board with cornflour and place your rolled icing on it. Let the icing dry slightly.

Lay the paper template on top of the icing and trace the outline of the skull, then lift off the paper. Using a craft knife, cut the skull and crossbones shape out of the icing. Stick them on the cake with a dab of water.

For the bandana, follow the instructions on how to trace and cut out a shape as you did with the skull and crossbones.

Stick the bandana above the skull with a little water. For the little bandana knot flaps, use the remaining red icing to cut out a 6 x 4 cm (2½ x 1½ in) strip. Cut the long side on a 45° angle to make two triangles (step 4).

Pinch the short side of the triangles into a few pleats and trim the edges. Stick both pleated triangles on the right side of the bandana with a little water (step 6).

Decorate the side
For the cutlasses, knead the grey icing to a pliable consistency, and then roll it to 3 mm (⅛ in) thick.

Follow the instructions on how to trace and cut out a shape as you did with the skull and crossbones. Paint the cutlasses with silver dust and stick them on the cake, while they are still soft, with a little water (page 61).

For the handles, roll a small sausage of black icing and mould it into two handles. Stick the handles on the cake at the end of the blade with a little water (step 6).

For the stars, knead the yellow icing to a pliable consistency then roll out to 3 mm (⅛ in) thick. Using different-sized cutters, cut out stars and stick them on the side of the cake with a little water, placing them at random.

Base seam
Knead the 200 g (7 oz) of red icing to a pliable consistency. Using an icing smoother, roll the icing into a roll (page 62). Brush a line of water on the base around the cake and carefully roll the cord around it, starting at the back. Roll a small ball out of the remaining red icing to cover the join.

The present box is a wonderfully simple idea that looks great in any colour, or combination of colours. This cake introduces you to a number of techniques, such as making a bow and a lid and creating stripes.

Present box cake

Materials
22 cm (9 in) round cake
100 ml (3½ fl oz) syrup
1.5 kg (3 lb 5 oz) ganache
1.5 kg (3 lb 5 oz) white icing (cake)
600 g (1 lb 5 oz) white icing (board)
600 g (1 lb 5 oz) blue icing (lid and strips)
500 g (1 lb 2 oz) white icing (strips and ribbon)
200 g (7 oz) white icing (seam)
250 g (9 oz) white icing (bow)
20 g (¾ oz) white icing (tag/ optional)
50 g (1¾) blue royal icing (tag/ optional)

Equipment
Ganaching tools (page 14)
22 cm (9 in) round board (set-up)
35 cm (14 in) round board (display)
Large and small rolling pins
Cranked palette knife
Plastic sheets
Smoothers
Flexi-scraper
Pastry brush
Paintbrush
Small knife
Pizza wheel
Pasta machine
No. 2 piping tip

Prepare the cake
Follow the instructions on how to prepare and ganache a round cake (page 38).

Cover the cake
Knead the white icing for the cake to a pliable dough and roll out to 3 mm (⅛ in) thick, using a large rolling pin. Follow the instructions on how to cover a round cake (page 44).

Cover the display board
Knead the white icing for the board to a pliable dough and roll to 3 mm (⅛ in) thick. Follow the instructions on how to cover a board, using either method (page 48).

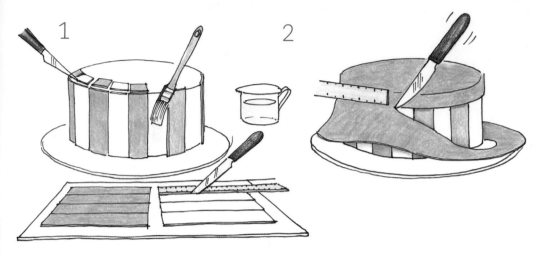

1. Cover the cake and board. Add strips of icing to the side of the cake.

2. Use a ruler to mark the edge of the lid all around the cake.

3. Place measured icing strips across the cake.

4. Make a thin icing roll to cover the base.

5. Prepare the bow and tag. Use tissue paper to keep the bow in shape until dry.

6. Attach the bow and tag.

To create soft, elegant bow loops, fill them with cotton wool and remove when the icing has dried.

Make the ribbon

Knead 250 g (9 oz) of the white icing to a pliable dough and roll out to a 16 x 20 cm (6¼ x 8 in) rectangle. Cut the rectangle into four long 4 cm (1½ in) wide strips. Trim one end of each ribbon into a V shape to help join the ribbons at the top. Stick on the cake with water and trim excess ends with a knife (step 3).

Make the base seam

Knead the white icing for the seam into a pliable dough and roll it into a thin roll that is long enough to fit around the cake (page 62). Lay the icing roll around the base of the cake and trim at the joining line (step 4). Roll a little ball out of the remaining white icing and stick it onto the joining line with a little water.

Make the bow

Knead the white icing for the bow into a pliable dough. Follow the instructions on how to make a bow (page 58).

Make the tag (optional)

Make your own template to cut a rectangle out of the white icing and cut off two triangles on both sides to achieve a pointy side, using a small knife. Smooth the edges with your finger. Using the end of your piping tube, make a hole in the end of the tag (step 5). Bend the tag a little for a more realistic look. Allow the tag to dry and harden, then stick it on your cake. Using a no. 2 piping tip, pipe a name or word on the tag (page 56).

Place the bow and the tag

Place the bow on top of the cake on the joining line on top of the ribbon. Knead 20 g (¾ oz) of the leftover blue icing and then roll it thinly into a sausage. Thread the thin roll through the hole in the tag and attach it to the bow with a little water.

Make the strips

Measure the circumference of the cake, and divide it into equal parts. It needs to be an even number; for instance, if your cake is 28 cm (11 in) in circumference, each of the strips should be 1 cm (½ in) wide. Roll out 250 g (9 oz) of the blue and 250 g (9 oz) of the 500 g (1 lb 2 oz) white icing to 3 mm (⅛ in) thick.

Use a pizza wheel or a sharp small knife to cut ten 3 cm (1¼ in) wide strips in blue and ten matching strips in white, to a length that is approximately the height of the cake. Cover the strips with plastic to prevent the icing drying out.

Using a paintbrush dampened with water (or syrup), brush a small line on the cake to make the icing sticky (page 54).

Stick the first strip on the cake, starting from the bottom edge and moving up to the top. Trim the top end of the strip with a knife (step 1). Repeat, alternating the colour, until all the strips are placed on the cake.

Make the lid

Let the cake sit for a couple of hours to allow the icing to dry before you make the lid.

Brush the top of the cake with a little water (or syrup) and run the brush around the top 2.5 cm (1 in) of the side of the cake.

Knead 300 g (10½ oz) of the blue icing to a pliable dough. Roll the icing to at least 20 cm (8 in) larger than the diameter of the cake. Roll the icing over your rolling pin, lift it up and roll it over the cake. Smooth the top and sides with a flexi-scraper. Use a ruler to mark the edge of the lid all around the side of the cake (step 2).

Make sure the ruler mark is lower than the water line, otherwise the icing will be sloppy below the line of the lid. Trim the lid with a sharp clean knife.

I can think of a lot of adults who would love this cake — and with the colour and name changed it could also be made for a king or queen. The princess cake introduces you to frilling, cut-outs, piping and painting in gold.

Princess cake

Materials
22 cm (9 in) round cake
100 ml (3½ fl oz) syrup
1.5 kg (3 lb 5 oz) ganache
1.2 kg (2 lb 10 oz) pink icing (cake)
1.1 kg (2 lb 7 oz) white icing (board, collar, crown and letters)
Gold cachous
250 g (9 oz) hot pink icing (seam)
Decorating alcohol
100 g (3½ oz) white royal icing
Edible gold dust

Equipment
Ganaching tools (page 14)
22 cm (9 in) round board (set-up)
35 cm (14 in) round board (display)
18 cm (7 in) round board (template)
Large and small rolling pins
Plastic scraper
Cranked palette knife
Smoothers
Serrated knife
Flexi-scraper
Plastic sheets
Frilling tool (or cocktail stick)
Paintbrush
Piping bag
No. 1 and no. 2 piping tips
Alphabet cutters
Pasta machine
Baking paper
2B pencil

Prepare the cake
Follow the instructions on how to prepare and ganache a round cake (page 38).

Cover the cake
Knead the pink icing to a pliable dough and roll to 3 mm (⅛ in) thick. Follow the instructions on how to cover a round cake (page 44).

Cover the display board
Knead 700 g (1 lb 9 oz) of the white icing to a pliable dough. Follow the instructions on how to cover a round board, using either method (page 48).

Decorate the side with cachous
Straight after covering the cake and while the icing is still soft, make small indents in the side of the cake

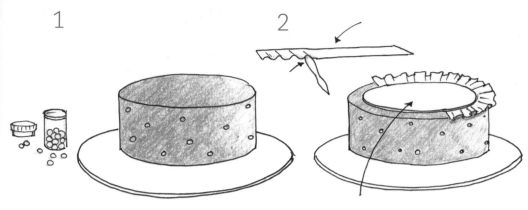

1
2

1. Cover the prepared and ganached cake and board.

2. Attach the frilled collar.

3. Roll little balls of icing and place them around the base of the cake.

4. Pipe the design on the crown and paint.

5. Paint the rolled icing and cut out the letters.

6. Place the crown and lettering on the cake.

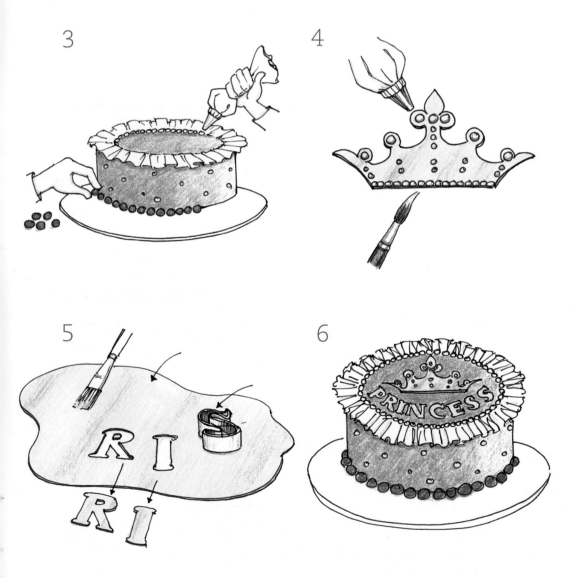

3
4
5
6

in a random pattern, using a frilling tool. Press the cachous carefully into the indents (step 1). Use the flexi-scraper to smooth the side of the cake so the cachous sit flush with the icing.

Note: If the icing is not soft and the cachous don't stay on it, you can stick them on with a little royal icing.

Make the frilled collar
Knead 200 g (7 oz) of the white icing into a pliable dough and roll to 3 mm (⅛ in) thick.

Using a pizza wheel cut out two strips of about 3 cm (1¼ in) wide and about 30 cm (12 in) long. Cover the icing strips with a plastic sheet to prevent them from drying out.

Place one of the strips on a clean work surface lightly dusted with cornflour and, using a frilling tool or a stick, roll along the side of the strip. Roll the tool back and forth to thin out the icing to achieve a frilly look (page 61). Brush a fine line of water around the top edge of the cake. Place the template board on the cake as a guide for the frilled collar (step 2). Stick the first frilled strip on the water line while pleating the icing with your fingers to get a fabric effect (step 2). Repeat with the second strip and join the frilly strips by overlapping the ends.

Make the balls for the base seam
Knead the hot pink icing to a pliable dough. Roll out a strip to about the thickness of your little finger and to about 30 cm (12 in) long. Cut the roll into about 50 slices in two different sizes. Keep the icing covered with plastic to prevent it from drying out.

Run a line of water around the bottom edge of the cake. Roll the icing pieces into balls varying in size and place them next to each other on the side of the cake in a random pattern (step 3).

The charm of this cake lies in the delicacy of the frill and the beautifully decorated crown. Instead of using alphabet cutters you could pipe a name or word on the cake.

Pipe along the frilled collar
Fill a piping bag with a no. 2 tip with white royal icing. Pipe little dots around the inner edge of the frilled collar on top of the cake to cover the joining line (step 3). Follow the instructions on how to pipe (page 56).

Make the crown
Enlarge the crown template (page 186), trace on baking paper and cut it out.

Knead 100 g (3½ oz) of the white icing to a pliable dough and roll out to 5 mm (¼ in) thick. Place the template on the icing and cut around it. Take the template off and smooth the edges with your finger. Use a piping bag, filled with white royal icing, with a no. 2 tip. Pipe little dots on the crown to create an attractive pattern. Let the royal icing dry, then paint the crown with gold dust mixed with decorating alcohol. While the colour is still wet, stick golden cachous on it for decoration (step 4).

Make the letters
Knead 100 g (3½ oz) of the white icing to a pliable dough. Roll to 5 mm (¼ in) thick, using a pasta machine or a rolling pin. Let the icing dry, then paint it with gold dust mixed with decorating alcohol. Let it dry, then cut out the letters you need for the word or name you want to put on your cake (step 5).

Smooth the edges of the letters with your fingertip, and then stick the letters on the cake with a little water.

Tip: If you don't have alphabet cutters create your own letters and trace them on a piece of paper or cardboard and cut them out. Use the same process as for making the crown.

Place the crown and letters
Once the crown and letters are dry, carefully lift them up and stick them on the cake using a little water (step 6).

If you have any apprehensions at all about your skills, the lollipop cake makes a fantastic place to start. The techniques and decorations consist of nothing more complicated than colouring icing and creating rolls and a bow, yet the results are stunning.

Lollipop cake

Materials
22 cm (9 in) round cake
100 ml (3½ fl oz) syrup
1.5 kg (3 lb 5 oz) ganache
1 kg (2 lb 4 oz) pink icing (cake)
1.2 kg (2 lb 12 oz) white icing (board)
200 g (7 oz) yellow icing (coil)
200 g (7 oz) pink icing (coil)
50 g (1¾ oz) green icing (coil)
50 g (1¾ oz) blue icing (coil)
300 g (10½ oz) caramel icing (stick)
400 g (14 oz) red icing (bow)

Equipment
Ganaching tools (page 14)
2 x 22 cm (9 in) round boards (set-up)
46 x 30 cm (18 x 12 in) rectangular cake board (display)
Large and small rolling pins
Plastic scraper
Cranked palette knife
Smoothers
Serrated knife
Small sharp kitchen knife
Flexi-scraper
Pastry brush
Plastic sheets
Paintbrush
Pasta machine

Prepare the cake
Follow the instructions on how to prepare and ganache a round cake (page 38).

Cover the cake
Knead the pink icing to a pliable dough and roll to 3 mm (⅛ in) thick. Follow the instructions on how to cover a round cake (page 44).

Cover the display board
Knead the white icing to a pliable dough and roll to 3 mm (⅛ in) thick, using a large rolling pin. Follow the instructions on how to cover a board (page 48).

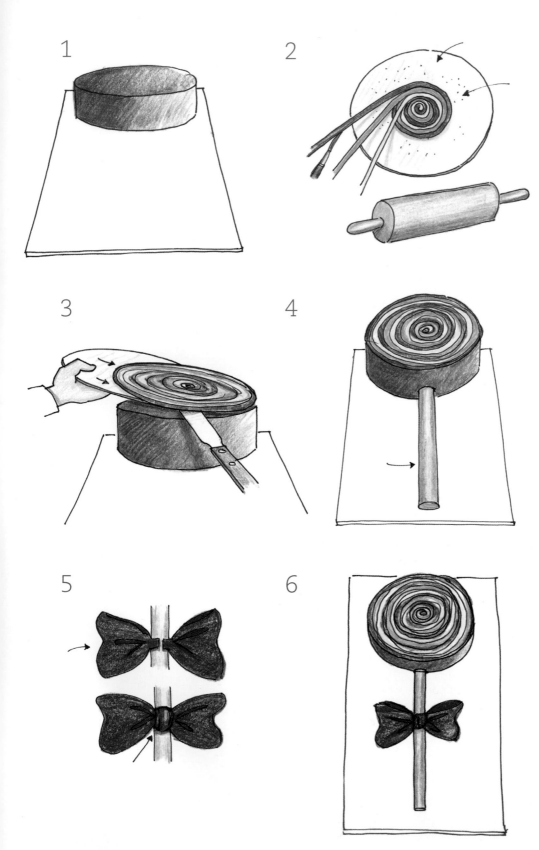

1. Cover the cake and position at one end of the board, leaving the other end free for the stick.

2. Coil the four colours together on a round board and roll flat.

3. Slide the coil onto the cake.

4. Position the stick.

5. Make the bow and attach it on the stick.

6. Add the finishing touches.

The appeal of this cake lies in the fact that the stripes don't have to be absolutely perfect.

Lollipop colours

Knead the four coloured lollipop icings individually to a pliable dough, using a little cornflour on the work surface, if needed. Use a rolling pin to roll out each colour to a strip about the thickness of your index finger. Use an acrylic smoother to create an even roll (page 62) and then cover with plastic. Roll all the colours to the same length, including the smaller quantities (these rolls will be thinner). Start rolling all four cords into a coil on a 22 cm (9 in) round board. Roll the huge coil flat until it fills the whole board (step 2). Slide the coil onto the cake (step 3). Lift the coil carefully and brush the cake with water so the coil sticks.

Lollipop stick

Knead the caramel icing to a pliable dough and roll it out to about 20 cm (8 in) long. Stick it onto the board at the bottom of the lollipop with a little water (step 4).

Make the bow

Knead the red icing to a pliable dough. Follow the instructions on how to make a bow (page 58).

Place the bow

Stick one loop of the bow on the board with a little water, right next to the lollipop stick, about halfway down. Repeat with the second bow loop, sticking it on the other side of the lollipop stick.

Pleat the square piece of icing into a few folds, making sure the raw edge is positioned on the inside (step 5). Stick the pleated icing onto the lollipop stick between the two bow loops so it looks like a bow tied around the stick (steps 5+6).

Square cakes

So now you've progressed from round cakes to squares and rectangles. The tricky bit of decorating cakes with angles is knowing what to do with all that icing when you reach the corners.

This cake can be made even easier by keeping the sails a plain colour rather than colouring them with spots and stripes. This cake shows the effectiveness of cut-outs and simple modelling.

Boat cake

Materials
250 g (9 oz) white icing (sails)
250 g (9 oz) blue icing (sails)
4 wooden skewers
Piping gel
1 cm (½ in) satin ribbon (flags)
300 g (10½ oz) white icing
 (spinnakers)
100 g (3½ oz) blue icing (spots)
100 g (3½ oz) yellow icing (spots)
100 g (3½ oz) white icing (boats)
20 cm (8 in) square cake
100 ml (3½ fl oz) syrup
1.5 kg (3 lb 5 oz) ganache
1.5 kg (3 lb 5 oz) light blue icing
 (cake)
1 kg (2 lb 4 oz) blue icing (board and
 wave)
200 g (7 oz) red icing (buoy)
200 g (7 oz) white icing (buoy and
 rope)

Equipment
35 cm (14 in) square board (display)
20 cm (8 in) square board (set-up)
Large and small rolling pins
Pasta machine
Baking paper
Pizza wheel
Paintbrushes
Plastic sheets
Hot glue (optional)
Glue gun (optional)
Set of circle cutters
Ganaching tools (page 14)
Smoothers
Flexi-scraper
Ruler
Scissors

Make the sails
Enlarge the template (page 188) with a photocopier. Trace on baking paper and cut it out. Roll out the white and blue icing into large squares 5 mm (¼ in) thick. Cut the icing into 1 cm (½ in) wide strips, then glue the alternate colours together with a paintbrush and a thin line of water (step 1).

Roll over the icing with a rolling pin so that the strips come together. Place your template on top to make sure you can cut four sails out of the strips (step 1, page 116). Leave until it has dried a little but is still soft.

Use the template to cut out the sail. Stick the sail to a skewer with piping gel, leaving room for the flag at the top. Leave to dry.

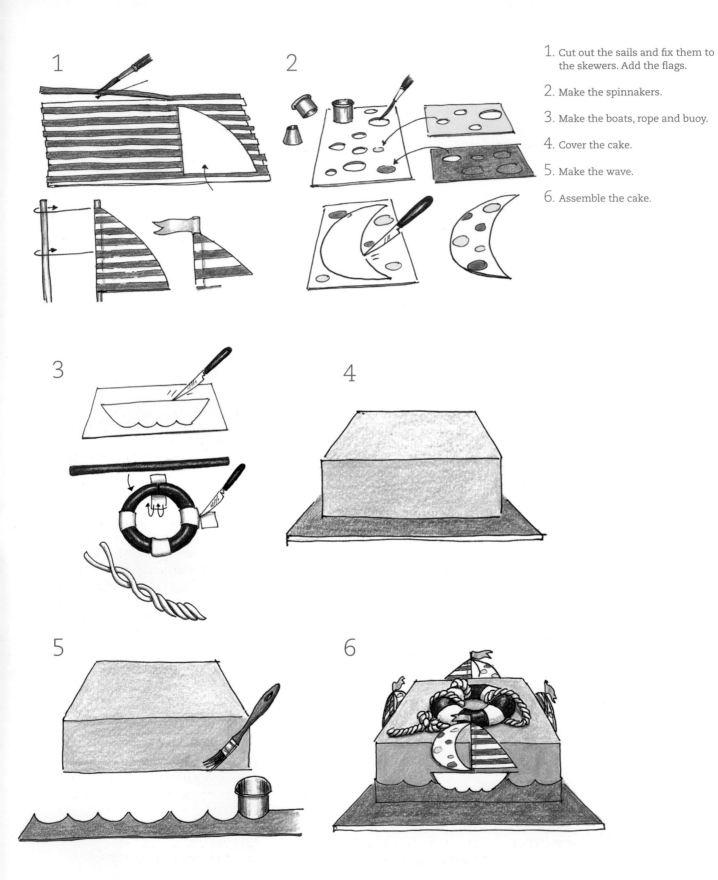

1. Cut out the sails and fix them to the skewers. Add the flags.

2. Make the spinnakers.

3. Make the boats, rope and buoy.

4. Cover the cake.

5. Make the wave.

6. Assemble the cake.

If you want to personalise the cake you can pipe a name onto the boats before you stick them on the cake.

Trim the skewer to size. Cut flags from the satin ribbon and glue to the top of the skewer using a hot glue gun. Repeat to make four sails.

Make the spinnakers
Roll out the white icing to 3 mm (⅛ in) thick and large enough to cut out four spinnakers. Roll out the blue and yellow icings to 3 mm (⅛ in). Use 2–3 small circle cutters or piping tips to cut out circles in the white icing and replace them with the same size circles from the yellow and blue icings (step 2).

Roll over the decorated icing very lightly with a rolling pin and cut out the spinnaker shapes using the template. Set aside to harden.

Make the boats
Roll out the white icing to 5 mm (¼ in) thick and large enough to cut out four boats. Place the template on the icing and cut around the outlines (step 3). Set aside and allow to harden.

Prepare the cake
Follow the instructions on how to prepare and ganache a square cake (page 37).

Cover the cake
Knead the light blue icing to a pliable dough and roll out to 3 mm (⅛ in) thick. Follow the instructions on how to cover a square cake (page 46).

Make the wave border
Roll out 200 g (7 oz) of the blue icing to 3 mm (⅛ in) thick. Use a ruler and a pizza wheel to cut a 4 cm (1½ in) wide rectangular strip long enough to wrap around the cake. Working quickly so the icing does not dry, use a 1 cm (½ in) circle cutter to cut out semi-circles from the top border to create the wave effect. Lightly brush around the base of the cake with water to stick the border on (step 5). Roll the wave border onto a small rolling pin and unroll around the sides of the cake, smoothing and pressing as you go.

Make the rope and buoy
Follow the instructions on how to make an icing roll (page 62). Roll 150 g (5½ oz) of the white icing into two 30 cm (12 in) long rolls. Twist the rolls to make the rope. Make a thick red roll. Join the ends and stick them together with a little water. Roll out the remaining white icing to 3 mm (⅛ in), cut four small white strips to decorate the red ring. Wrap the squares around the ring, making sure to cover the join (step 3).

Cover the display board
Knead the remaining blue icing to a pliable dough. Roll to 3 mm (⅛ in) thick. Follow the instructions on how to cover a board (page 48).

Assemble the cake
Arrange the buoy and rope on the cake before the rope hardens. Stick the boats on with a little water, leaving enough room for the sails. Stick the trimmed skewers on the cake, then stick on the spinnakers.

I love this cake design because it's so versatile. Once you've mastered the blueprint you can create suitcases, beauty cases and laptop bags. You could make luggage labels or address tags. If you're a beginner, simplify the design by making the handle from solid icing only and using a single colour for the tie.

Briefcase cake

Materials
20 cm (8 in) square cake
30 cm (12 in) aquarium tube
450 g dark brown icing (handle and attachements)
Piping gel
200 g (10½ oz) dark brown icing (decoration)
100 ml (3½ fl oz) syrup
1.5 kg (3 lb 5 oz) ganache
1.5 kg (3 lb 5 oz) brown icing (cake)
1 kg (2 lb 4 oz) white icing (board)
300 g (10½ oz) caramel icing (gold detail)
Edible gold dust
Decorating alcohol
350 g (12 oz) red icing (tie)
350 g (12 oz) white icing (tie)
350 g (12 oz) blue icing (tie)
50 g royal icing

Equipment
30 x 20 cm (12 in x 8 in) board (set-up)
40 cm (16 in) square board (display)
Baking paper
2B pencil
Small kitchen or paring knife
2 wooden skewers or dowels
Paintbrushes
Cornflour
Large and small rolling pins
Scissors
Plastic sheets
Flexi-scraper
Stitching tool
Ganaching tools (page 14)
2 smoothers
Ruler
Set of circle cutters
Frilling tool

Make the handle
This method will give the handle a very realistic look. A less fiddly way is to make it from solid icing. Follow the same instructions but replace the tubes with a sausage of 100 g (3½ oz) dark brown icing and allow extra time for drying.

Enlarge the template (page 187) with a photocopier, trace on baking paper and cut it out. Place a skewer in each end of the tubing, making sure it is long enough to insert into the cake. If the skewers are loose, insert a few toothpicks to tighten. Brush the tube with piping gel.

To cover the tube, roll out 150 g (5½ oz) of the dark brown icing to 3 mm (⅛ in) thick and cut into a rectangle large enough to fold over the handle, allowing for some overhang of about 1 cm (½ in). Trim off the excess icing and smooth down the seam with your fingers.

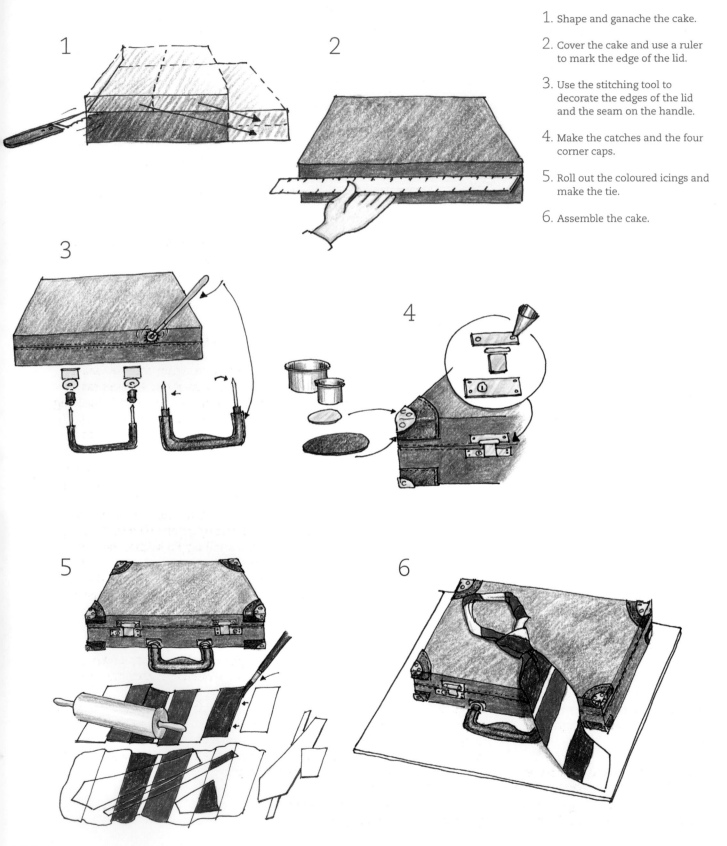

1. Shape and ganache the cake.

2. Cover the cake and use a ruler to mark the edge of the lid.

3. Use the stitching tool to decorate the edges of the lid and the seam on the handle.

4. Make the catches and the four corner caps.

5. Roll out the coloured icings and make the tie.

6. Assemble the cake.

1

2

3

4

5

6

Then roll 200 g (7 oz) of the dark brown icing to 3 mm (⅛ in) thick. Use your template to cut out two pieces of dark brown icing. Cover with plastic to prevent drying out. Brush the covered handle with water and stick the two pieces on top. Smooth the joining line with your fingers. With a stitching tool or a toothpick, stitch marks along the sides of the handle.

Make the handle attachments
Roll out the remaining dark brown icing to make a small cylinder about 4 cm (1½ in) long and 2 cm (¾ in) in diameter. Cut the cylinder in half crossways and stick on the skewers at the base of the handle (step 3).

Prepare the cake
Follow the instructions on how to make and ganache a 30 x 20 cm (12 x 8 in) rectangular cake (page 40). Place the cake on the set-up board.

Cover the cake
Knead the brown icing to a pliable dough and roll out to 3 mm (⅛ in) thick. Follow the instructions on how to cover a square cake (page 46). Quickly move to the next step while the icing is still soft.

Cover the display board
Follow the instructions on how to cover a board (page 48). Place the cake onto the board.

Indent the lid
To create the lid, mark a line around the sides of the cake about one-third from the top using a ruler. Mark both sides of the line with the stitching tool (steps 2+3).

Make the catches and the corners
For the catches, roll out 200 g (7 oz) of the caramel icing to 3 mm (⅛ in) and cut the shapes. Stick

Paint the buckles and catches in gold to give them a realistic look.

them on the cake with a bit of water. Make four small balls and stick them underneath the corners as leg rests.

For the corners, roll out 200 g (7 oz) of the dark brown icing to 3 mm (⅛ in) and cut out two large circles of 8 cm (3¼ in) in diameter with a circle cutter. Cut the circles in half and place one on each corner of the lid with a dab of water.

Cut out four rectangles to the diameter of the circles and about 2 cm (¾ in) wide. Stick on the base corners with a dab of water. Mark each corner cap with the stitching tool (step 4).

To create the base of the gold detail on each corner, cut out six circles from the caramel icing with a 6 cm (2½ in) circle cutter, then cut two of these in half for the bottom corners. Place a full circle on the corners of the lid with a dab of water and do the same with the half circles for the bottom corners.

Create the screws on the smaller circles with a no. 2 piping tip.

Make the handle base
To create the gold detail at the base of the handle, roll out the caramel icing to about 3 mm (⅛ in) and cut two squares about the size of postage stamps. Then make two thick discs slightly smaller than the squares. Use the handle as a guide to help you place the bases in the correct position. Stick them to the briefcase with a dab of water, placing the discs on top of the squares (step 3).

Paint the buckles and corner caps with gold powder mixed with decorating alcohol (page 61).

Push the handle into the lower side of the front of the cake and let it rest on the board.

Make and place the tie
Enlarge the tie template (page 187) with a photocopier, trace on baking paper and cut it out. Roll out two strips of the red, white and blue icing into large rectangles 5 mm (¼ in) thick, using your tie template as a guide for the width required (step 5).

Use a pizza wheel or sharp knife to cut the three icings into thin strips and then glue the alternate colours together with a paintbrush and a thin line of water. Roll over the icing with a rolling pin so that the strips come together. Leave until it has dried a little but is still soft. Place the template on top of the icing and cut out the tie, knot and neckpiece (step 5).

Fold the neckpiece in half lenghtways, form a loop and place it on the briefcase. Pinch the top of the tie to create creases and stick it on the joining line under the tie loop on the briefcase. Wrap the tie knot around it to cover the joining lines. Secure the tie with a brush of water (step 6).

This cake design using wire decorations can easily be adapted to just about any occasion. For Valentine's Day, change the colour and use hearts instead of stars. (We've even been asked to make this with flying pigs on the wires!)

Exploding star cake

Material
20 cm (8 in) square cake
100 ml (3½ fl oz) syrup
1.5 kg (3 lb 5 oz) ganache
2 x 30 g (1 oz) green icing (stars)
2 x 30 g (1 oz) yellow icing (stars)
2 x 30 g (1 oz) red icing (stars)
2 x 30 g (1 oz) light blue icing (stars)
100 g (3½ oz) orange icing
   (numbers)
2 x 30 g (1 oz) red icing
   (explosion rip)
1.5 kg (3 lb 5 oz) blue icing (cake)
600 g black icing (board)
150 g (5½ oz) red icing (ribbon)
100 g (3½ oz) orange icing (seam)
Silver cachous

Equipment
20 cm (8 in) square board (set-up)
35 cm (14 in) square board (display)
Ganaching tools (page 14)
20 x 40 cm (16 in) no. 22 gauge wire
Wire cutters (secateurs)
Cornflour
Large and small rolling pins
Star cutters
Plastic sheet
Paintbrushes
Smoothers
Flexi-scraper
Frilling tool
Pastry brush
Set of circle cutter
Number cutters (or DIY template)
Pasta machine
Ruler

Prepare the cake
Follow the instructions on how to prepare and ganache a square cake (page 39).

Make the stars and numbers
To make the stars, roll out one portion of the star colours to 3 mm (⅛ in) thick. Use star cutters to cut out 15 to 20 different-sized stars. Cover with plastic. Stick the end of the wires into water and push into the stars. Let dry on a flat surface. For the numbers, roll out the orange icing to 5 mm (¼ in). Cut out the numbers. Stick two more wires into water and push into each number. Let dry on a flat surface. Trim the wires to differentiate them in height from the stars (step 1, page 124).

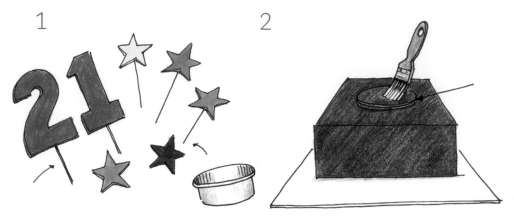

1
2

1. Make the stars and numbers.

2. Create the explosion rip.

3. Cover the cake and cut the rip.

4. Fold back the triangles and add the ribbon.

5. Decorate the sides with stars and some cachous.

6. Place stars and numbers.

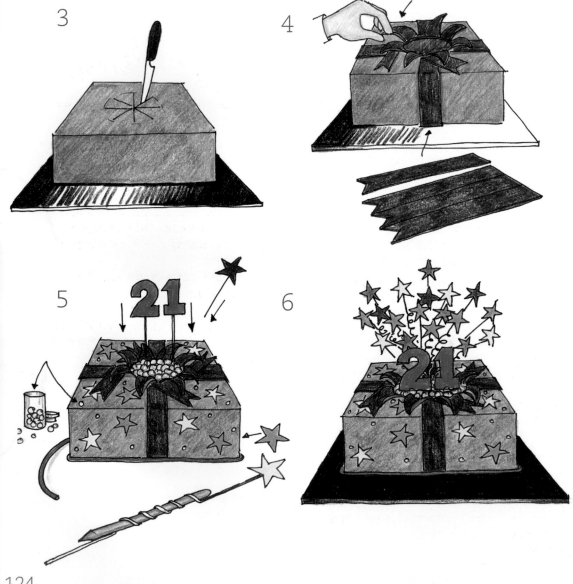

Create the explosion rip

Read the instructions on how to cover a square cake (page 46) before you start.

Brush your cake with syrup. Roll out each explosion rip icing piece to 3 mm (⅛ in) thick. Use an 8 cm (3¼ in) circle cutter to cut out two circles. Place the circles on top of each other in the centre of the cake and brush only the top of the top circle with syrup (step 2).

Cover the cake

Knead the blue icing to a pliable dough. Roll to 3 mm (⅛ in) thick and follow the instructions on how to cover a square cake. With a small knife, cut four lines through the blue icing and into the circle so you end up with eight triangles (take care to cut only through the top circle and not through to the cake). Pull the triangles outwards so they curl back like a flower, exposing the colour underneath (steps 3+4).

Make the ribbon

Roll the red icing in the pasta machine or by hand to 3 mm (⅛ in) thick. Use a ruler and pizza wheel to cut four strips about 20 cm (8 in) long and 2.5 cm (1 in) wide.

Cut a V into one end of each strip. Cover with a plastic sheet to prevent it drying out (step 4).

Brush a line of water on all four sides of the cake and stick the strips on. Starting from the top, curl the strips back just under the explosion rip to create the effect of a present that has just been opened.

Take the strips along the side of the cake and trim flush on the base with a sharp knife.

Cover the display board

Roll out the black icing to 3 mm (⅛ in) thick. Follow the instructions on how to cover a board (page 48).

This cake is great for anniversaries and birthday parties. With a set of number cutters you are able to create any number you want.

Make the decorative stars

Roll out the remaining portions of the star colours to 3 mm (⅛ in). Cut out the stars and cover with plastic to prevent them from drying out. Stick half of the stars in a random pattern on the cake with water.

With a frilling tool, poke indentations in the sides of the cake and place cachous. Polish with the flexi-scraper.

Tip: The stars can be used to cover any cracks in the icing.

Cover the base seams

Knead the orange icing to a pliable consistency and then, using an acrylic smoother, roll it into a roll (page 62). Brush a line of water along the base of the cake and carefully roll the cord around it, starting at the back. Cover the joining line with a ball of icing.

Place the stars and numbers

Wind the wire of the stars around a pencil, then pull out the pencil. Be careful not to damage the stars. Arrange the stars and numbers on the cake just as you would a bunch of flowers.

Fill the explosion rip with the silver cachous.

Tip: Create as much height variation as possible by trimming the wires.

This cake is quite fiddly — rather than cutters and templates, you'll need your modelling skills for creating the turntable arm and knobs. When you start creating realistic cakes like this, if you don't have a real record player to look at it's always helpful to have a photo to work from.

Record player cake

Materials
25 cm (10 in) square cake (see Note)
100 ml (3½ fl oz) syrup
1.5 kg (3 lb 5 oz) ganache
1.5 kg (3 lb 5 oz) orange icing (cake)
600 g (1 lb 5 oz) grey icing (turntable and shifter)
50 g (1¾ oz) blue icing (knobs)
1 x 5 mm (¼ in) wooden dowel
Edible silver dust
Decorating alcohol
700 g (1 lb 9 oz) white icing (board)
18 cm (7 in) length 5 mm (¼ in) wooden dowel (arm)
Piping gel
1 x no. 20 (strength) gauge wire
100 g (3½ oz) black icing (record)
50 g (1¾ oz) red icing (record label)
200 g (7 oz) royal icing

Equipment
35 cm (14 in) square board (display)
25 cm (10 in) square board (set-up)
20 cm (8 in) round board (turntable template)
18 cm (7 in) round board (record template)
Ganaching tools (page 14)
Cornflour
Large and small rolling pins
Smoother
Waxed cardboard 6 x 2 cm (2½ x ¾ in) rectangle (DIY template)
Paintbrushes
Small kitchen knife
Pasta machine
Frilling tool
Flexi-scraper
No. 3 piping tip
Piping bag
Set of circle cutters
Set of oval cutters
Wire cutters (secateurs)
Pizza wheel

Shape and ganache the cake
This is a great trick to save you sculpting time. Use one of the 20 cm (8 in) square cake recipes and quantities but bake your cake in a 25 cm (10 in) cake tin. The cake will bake much lower, creating the size you want for the turntable shape which is 25 x 25 cm (10 x 10 in) and about 4 cm (1½ in) high. Slice the cake in half horizontally, then sandwich together with ganache. Follow the instructions on how to ganache a square cake (page 39).

Note: The cake will need about 10–15 minutes less time to bake in the bigger tin.

Cover the cake
Knead the orange icing to a pliable dough. Roll to 3 mm (⅛ in) thick and follow the instructions on how to cover a square cake (page 46).

Using a pastry brush for glazing the record will give it a nice shiny look as well as the typical record grooves.

Make the pitch shifter

While the icing is still soft, stamp the control for the pitch shifter at the far bottom right of the cake using the template (page 189). Use the back of a knife to make the impression down the centre (step 3).

Make the turntable

Roll out 300 g (10½ oz) of the grey icing to 1 cm (½ in) thick. Use the round 20 cm (8 in) cake board as a template to cut out the turntable. Place the icing circle on the board and cut around it, holding your knife at an angle to create a bevelled edge. Position the turntable towards the left side of the cake and stick it on with a little water. Use the frilling tool to create a pattern around the sides (step 2, page 131).

Glaze (optional)

Follow the instructions on how to glaze (page 54). Glaze the icing while it is still soft, using a pastry brush.

Make the knobs and player controls

Roll out 50 g (1¾ oz) of the blue and grey icings to 3 mm (⅛ in) thick. Create the knobs and controls using the piping tip and oval cutters (step 3). Cut out the smaller buttons with a piping tip. Cut out a larger blue circle and place a thin roll of icing around it. For the large cylindrical knob in the front, insert a wooden dowel and cover it with grey icing. Model it into shape using your fingers and with a flat knife create the flat sides. Stick the knobs and controls to the cake with a little water (step 4). Mix the edible silver dust with decorating alcohol and paint the knobs and controls. If you wish, you can paint the play buttons in black. Allow the silver to dry and mix black food colour and decorating alcohol and paint over the top, being careful not to smudge.

Cover the display board

Knead the white icing to a pliable dough. Follow the instructions on how to cover a board, using either method (page 48).

Using a very fine paintbrush, paint details such as for the play button and the volume control shifter.

Make the arm, arm holder, arm head and needle

For the arm, use an 18 cm (7 in) long wooden dowel and brush it with piping gel. Roll out 100 g (3½ oz) of the grey icing to 3 mm (⅛ in) thick. Cut a 18 x 1 cm (7 x ½ in) strip and wrap the icing around the gelled dowel. Trim the ends and let dry.

Roll out two thin 3 x 1 cm (1¼ x ½ in) strips of icing and wrap them around the arm using your fingers, smoothing and sticking them on with piping gel as you go. Trim, making sure the seam is underneath.

For the head and needle, use a bit of the leftover grey icing, the size of a walnut, and with your fingers and icing smoothers mould a needle head shape. Skewer it to the end of the record arm with piping gel and disguise the seam with a thin piece of icing or thin icing roll attached with piping gel. Trim the wire to a short piece and position it in the end of the record head. Allow to dry.

For the arm holder you will need to use your modelling skills as a lot of the details are created by hand. Roll out 150 g of the grey icing fairly thickly to 5 mm (¼ in) and cut out two circles with the cutters, the first about 6 cm (2½ in) and the second a bit smaller. Roll a cylinder to about 2.5 cm (1 in) long and about 3 cm (1¼ in) wide and model a hollow to create the arm holder (step 5). Use a piping tip to make indentations imitating screws (step 5). When all the elements are dry, mix edible silver dust with decorating alcohol and paint the arm, arm holder and arm head. Let dry.

Make the record

Roll out the black icing to about 5 mm (¼ in) thick and 20 cm (8 in) wide. Place the 18 cm (7 in) cake board on top and cut around it with a pizza wheel or a clean paring knife, making sure not to stretch the icing.

Roll out the red icing to about 3 mm (⅛ in) thick and cut out a circle with a 5 cm (2 in) diameter circle cutter. Place in the centre of the record with a dab of water. Use a piece of the wooden dowel to make the hole in the centre of the record. To create the central point in the turntable, roll a piece of grey icing into a cone with a flat base and paint silver. Leave the record and the cone to dry.

For the record grooves glaze the black icing while it is still soft, using a pastry brush (step 5).

Assemble the cake

Place the record on the turntable and adhere with some water, then use a pastry brush and piping gel to gel the top of the record.

Adhere the silver central piece with piping gel or water, taking care not to smudge.

Place the arm holder at the top right corner of the cake. Adhere together with royal icing, and use more royal icing to stick on the arm, positioning the needle on the record (step 6).

1. Cover the cake.

2. Make the turntable and position on the cake.

3. Make the knobs and controls.

4. Place the controls on the cake.

5. Make the record and the arm.

6. Add the finishing touches.

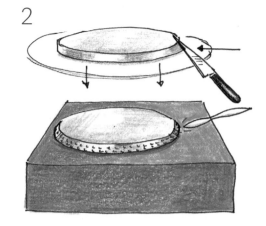

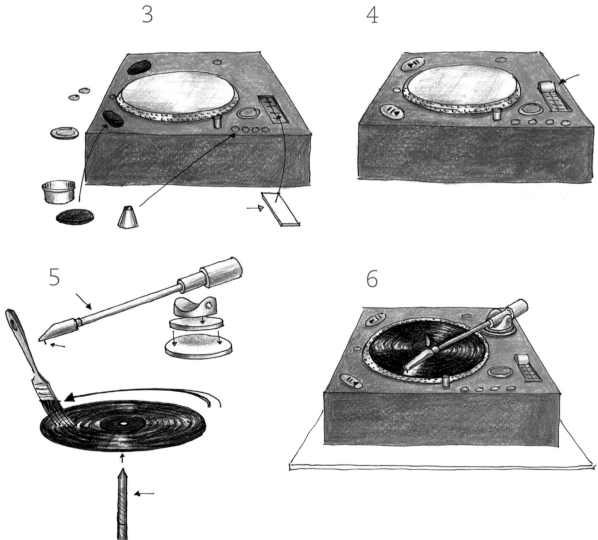

This cake is sure to amaze anyone who loves colour and make-up. Here, you'll be making your own template and make-up brushes, painting and creating a border.

Make-up box cake

Materials

20 cm (8 in) square cake
100 ml (3½ fl oz) syrup
1.5 kg (3 lb 5 oz) ganache
1.5 kg (3 lb 5 oz) mauve icing (cake)
200 g (7 oz) black icing (palette)
40 g (1½ oz) black icing (brushes)
20 g (¾ oz) pink icing (eyeshadow)
20g (¾ oz) aqua icing (eyeshadow)
20 g (¾ oz) blue icing (eyeshadow)
20 g (¾ oz) green icing (eyeshadow)
20 g (¾ oz) yellow icing (eyeshadow)
20g (¾ oz) red icing (blush)
20g (¾ oz) hot pink icing (blush)
20g (¾ oz) orange icing (blush)
20 g (¾ oz) brown icing (brush)
600 g (1 lb 5 oz) white icing (board)
Edible silver and lustre dust

Equipment

20 cm (8 in) square board (set-up)
35 cm (14 in) square board (display)
18 cm (7 in) square board
Ganaching tools (page 14)
Large and small rolling pins
Smoothers
Flexi-scraper
Waxed cardboard (stencil)
Set of circle cutters
Pasta machine
Plastic sheets
Small kitchen knife or paring knife
Ruler
Paintbrushes

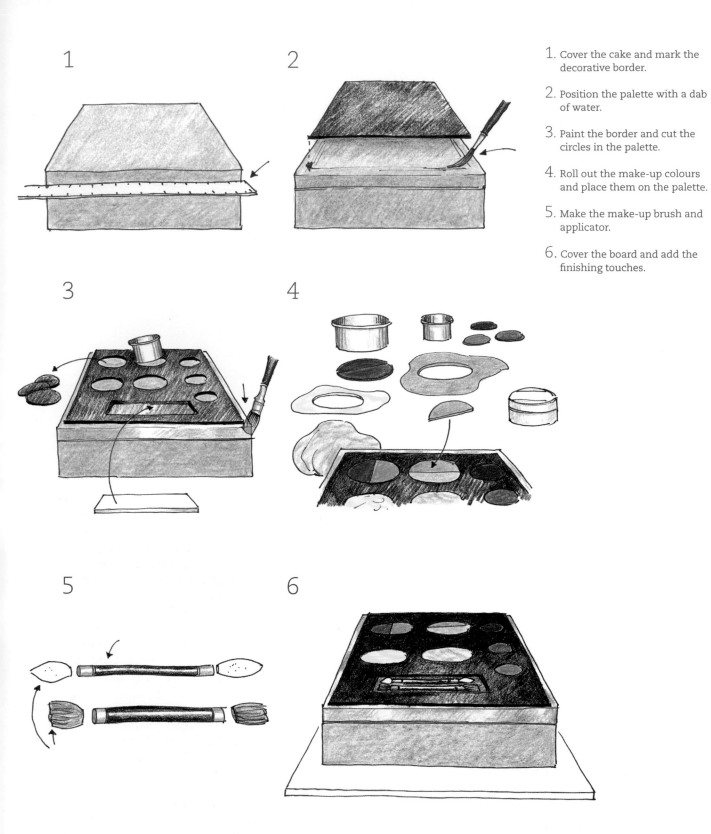

1. Cover the cake and mark the decorative border.

2. Position the palette with a dab of water.

3. Paint the border and cut the circles in the palette.

4. Roll out the make-up colours and place them on the palette.

5. Make the make-up brush and applicator.

6. Cover the board and add the finishing touches.

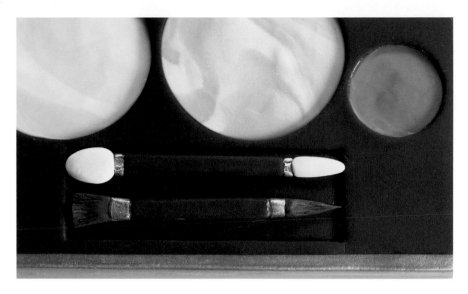

Use a small knife to mark the brush lines to achieve a realistic look.

Prepare the cake
Follow the instructions on how to prepare and ganache a square cake (page 39).

Cover the cake
Roll out the mauve icing to 3 mm (⅛ in) thick. Follow the instructions on how to cover a square cake (page 46).

For the decorative border, and while the icing is still soft, use a ruler to mark around the top of the sides of the cake (step 1). Mix together edible silver dust and decorating alcohol and paint the border with a paintbrush.

For the palette, use an 18 cm (7 in) square cake board as a template. Roll the black icing to 3 mm (⅛ in) and cut out a 18 cm (7 in) square. Place on the top of the cake with a dab of water around the edges only (step 2).

Make the make-up brush holder
Enlarge the template (page 186) with a photocopier, trace on baking paper and cut it out. While the icing is still soft use the template to stamp the make-up brush holder into the cake.

Be careful, you only get one chance to place this correctly. The indent does not need to be too deep.

Use a medium or large circle cutter to cut out four circles in the make-up palette and a small circle cutter to cut the three circles along the edge. Peel away the black icing (step 3).

Make the colours
Make the pink, aqua, blue, green, red, yellow and hot pink icings (or any colours you have chosen) and roll them to 3 mm (⅛ in) thick with a rolling pin or pasta machine.

Use the same circle cutters you used to create the palette to cut out the make-up colours, then cut two of them in half and mix and match (step 4). Brush lustre dust on the colours to enhance the look of the make-up.

Repeat these steps for the blush, using red, hot pink and orange icing. Place the make-up on the palette with a dab of water to secure them. Smooth over with a flexi-scraper.

Make the brush and applicator
For the brush, roll 20 g (¾ oz) of the black icing into a 5 mm (¼ in) thick and 12 cm (4½ in) long sausage tapered at one end. Use a bit of the brown icing about the size of a pea and shape it into a teardrop. Flatten it to get a brush-like shape then mark the brush lines. Glue the brush to the stick. Paint the front of the brush in edible silver dust mixed with decorating alcohol (page 61).

For the applicator, roll the remaining black icing into a 5 mm (¼ in) thick and 8 cm (3¼ in) long sausage tapered at both ends. Use a small amount of white icing (left-over from the board) and roll two balls. Flatten the balls to a teardrop and then stick on both ends of the black stick (step 5).

Cover the display board
Follow the instructions on how to cover a board, using either method (page 48).

Assemble the cake
Place the cake on the board and decorate with the make-up brushes and products.

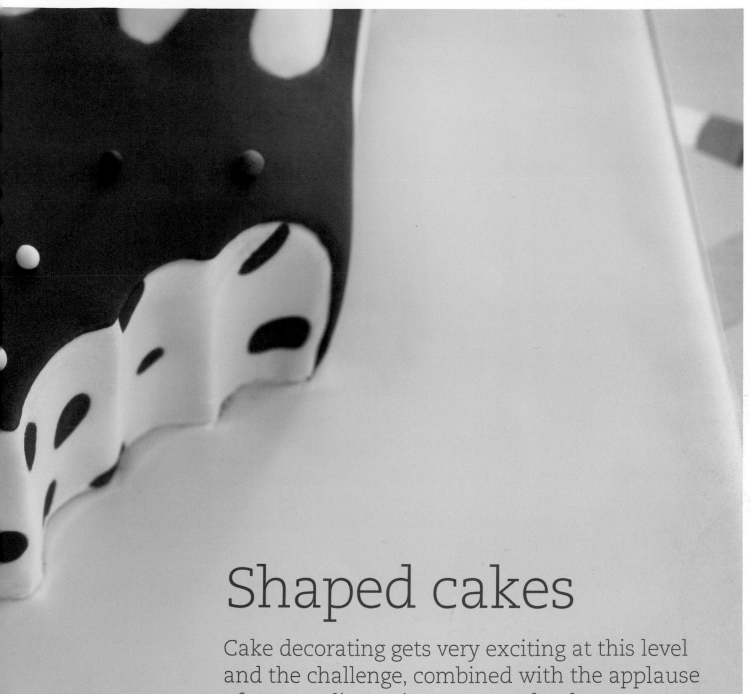

Shaped cakes

Cake decorating gets very exciting at this level and the challenge, combined with the applause of your audience, is guaranteed to keep you hooked. With most of these cakes, once you've mastered the basic concept, you can adapt the colours and designs to suit any occasion.

This is a truly versatile design and, once you've mastered the shape, it's really only limited by your imagination. Use the flag of a favourite sports team for Father's Day, or that of a country to celebrate a special trip.

Flag cake

Materials
20 cm (8 in) square cake
150 ml (5 fl oz) syrup
1.5 kg (3 lb 5 oz) ganache
1.2 kg (2 lb 10 oz) light blue icing (cake)
700 g (1 lb 9 oz) light blue icing (board)
150 g (5½ oz) orange icing (strips)
150 g (5½ oz) pink icing (strips)
150 g (5½ oz) blue icing (strips)
150 g (5½ oz) yellow icing (strips)
200 g (7 oz) brown icing (flagpole)
Edible glitter in pink
300 g (10½ oz) white icing (tassels)
Decorating alcohol
Royal icing
Edible gold dust

Equipment
40 cm (16 in) square cake board (display)
15 x 20 cm (6 x 8 in) rectangular DIY board
Serrated knife
Ganaching tools (page 14)
Cornflour
Large and small rolling pins
Plastic scraper
Smoothers
Flexi-scraper
Pastry brush
Pizza wheel
Pasta machine
Plastic sheets
Paintbrushes
Paring knife
Baking paper
2B pencil

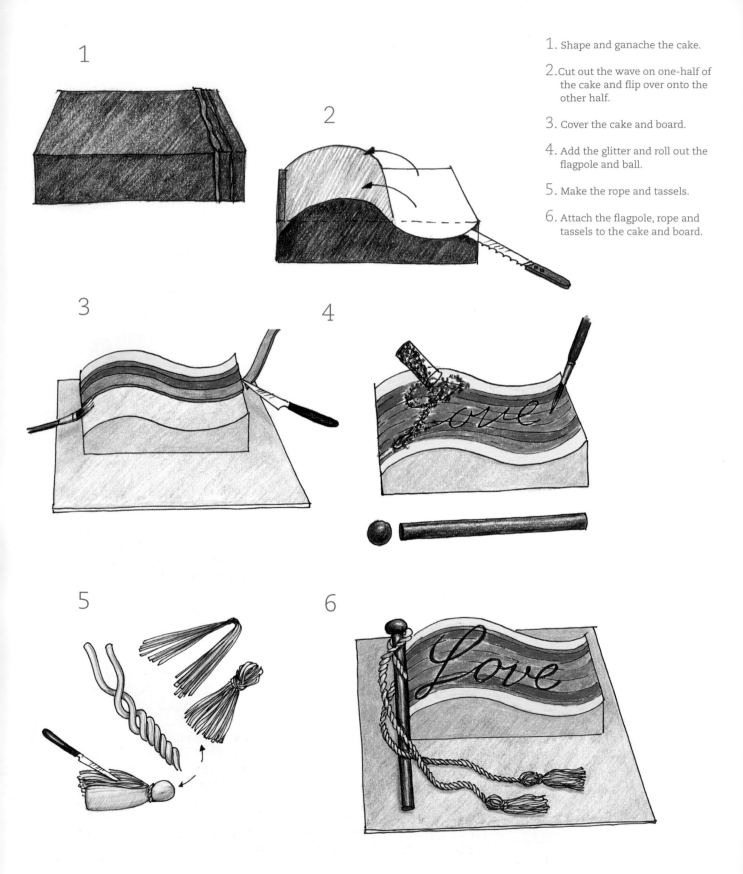

1

2

1. Shape and ganache the cake.

2. Cut out the wave on one-half of the cake and flip over onto the other half.

3. Cover the cake and board.

4. Add the glitter and roll out the flagpole and ball.

5. Make the rope and tassels.

6. Attach the flagpole, rope and tassels to the cake and board.

3

4

5

6

Mix gold dust with decorating alcohol and paint the tassels.

For the letters on the cake use a font you like and trace it on before you apply the glitter.

avoid staining it. Keep the strips covered with plastic.

Moisten the surface of the cake with a dab of water and place the strips on top, making sure the strips are as close together as possible (step 3). Manipulate the icing by pushing it to make it sit exactly on the cake. Quickly run the flexi-scraper over to smooth it. Using a sharp paring knife, trim the top to sit neatly at the sides (step 3).

Roll out the flagpole
Knead the brown icing to a pliable dough. On a work surface lightly dusted with cornflour, roll the brown icing into a 25 cm x 2. 5 cm (10 x 1 in) sausage. Use the cake smoother to roll it evenly (page 62). Place the flagpole with a little dab of water on the board next to the flag (step 6). With the remaining brown icing, roll a ball in the size of a walnut and place it on the top of the flagpole (steps 4+6).

Write with edible glitter
For the DIY template, find a font you like and make your own template (page 57). Stencil the lettering onto the cake. Using a fine paintbrush, trace over the lettering with syrup, sprinkle edible glitter onto the syrupy lettering and press gently to stick the glitter to the syrup. Let the glitter dry, then gently blow away any excess.

Make the rope and tassels
Use half the amount of the white icing for the tassels (page 55). For the rope, roll out two rolls (page 62) of the remaining white icing to 60 cm (24 in) in length and then twist together (step 5). Brush the rope and tassels with the edible gold dust (page 61). Allow to dry before attaching the rope and tassels on the board and around the flagpole (step 6).

Shape and ganache the cake
Trim 5 cm (2 in) from the side of the 20 cm (8 in) square and stick to a now shorter side with ganache, to get a 15 cm x 25 cm (6 x 10 in) rectangle (step 1). Using a long serrated knife, cut a moon shape from one half of your rectangle, but don't cut deeper than one third of the cake's depth. Flip the piece over onto the flat piece of the uncut rectangle and stick it on with ganache (step 2). Apply a little bit of ganache to the cake to seal the crumbs, and make sure the flag shape is perfect, before following the instructions on how to ganache a 30 x 20 cm (12 x 8 in) rectangular cake (page 40). Allow the ganache to set completely.

Cover the cake
Knead the blue icing to a pliable dough. Roll out to 3 mm ($\frac{1}{8}$ in) thick and follow the instructions on how to cover a shaped cake (page 47). Let sit for a couple of hours.

Cover the display board
Follow the instructions on how to cover a board, using either method (page 48). If you prefer to put the cake on a differently covered board, make sure the cake sits on a set-up board.

Make and arrange the flag strips
Roll out the coloured icing with a pasta machine or with a rolling pin to 3 mm ($\frac{1}{8}$ in) thick. Measure your cake and cut enough strips in different colours and widths to cover your cake, using a pizza wheel and a ruler. Make sure not to get any cornflour on top of the icing, to

141

This is smart, stylish and always a hit with adults and children alike. If you want to add more colour, pipe hundreds and thousands on the chocolate icing.

Ice-cream cake

Materials
20 cm (8 in) square cake
100 ml (3½ fl oz) syrup
1.2 kg (2 lb 10 oz) ganache
1 kg (2 lb 4 oz) pink icing (cake)
500 g (1 lb 2 oz) brown icing
    (chocolate dribbles)
700 g (1 lb 9 oz) white icing (board)
200 g (7 oz) caramel icing
    (ice-cream stick)

Equipment
30 x 20 cm (12 x 8 in) rectangular
    board (display)
Baking paper
2B pencil
Ganaching tools (page 14)
Pastry brush
Cornflour
Large and small rolling pins
Serrated knife
Plastic scraper
Smoothers
Flexi-scraper
Cranked palette knife
Pasta machine
Plastic sheets
Paintbrushes
Circle cutter (8 cm /3¼ in)

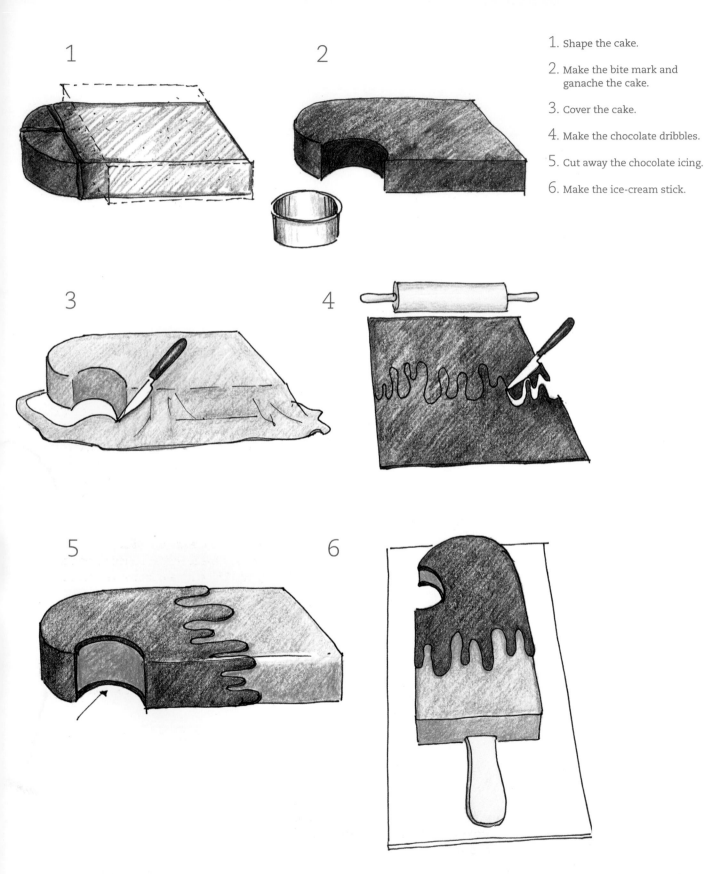

1
2

1. Shape the cake.

2. Make the bite mark and ganache the cake.

3. Cover the cake.

4. Make the chocolate dribbles.

5. Cut away the chocolate icing.

6. Make the ice-cream stick.

3
4

5
6

You can vary the design by adding more bite marks, using a slightly smaller circle cutter (design on page 136).

Shape the cake

Enlarge the ice-cream template (page 189) with a photocopier. Trace the template onto a sheet of baking paper and cut out.

Follow the instructions on how to cut a square into a rectangular cake (page 40).

Place the template on top of the rectangular cake and, with a small serrated knife, cut around it, making sure to keep the knife vertical to maintain a right-angle.

Place the cake on the board, leaving enough room for the ice-cream stick.

Make the bite mark and ganache the cake

Using the large circle cutter, cut out the bite mark (step 2). Follow the instructions on how to ganache a square cake (page 39). Allow to set before covering.

Cover the cake

Knead the pink icing to a pliable dough and roll to 3 mm (⅛ in) thick. Follow the instructions on how to cover a shaped cake (page 47).

Try to get the square edge of the ice-cream sharp and leave the sides slightly rounded. Allow the icing to dry before continuing (preferably overnight).

Make the chocolate dribbles

Enlarge the template for the ice-cream dribbles (page 189). Trace it onto baking paper and cut out. Roll out the brown icing to 3 mm (⅛ in) thick and large enough to cover half of the cake. Place the template on the icing, then cut out the dribbles using a paring knife (step 4). Dampen the cake where the brown icing is to go with a little water. Smooth the icing with a flexi-scraper and trim the base. Cut away the brown icing at the bite mark to expose the pink icing underneath and smooth the edges.

Cover the display board

Knead the white icing to a pliable dough and roll to 3 mm (⅛ in) thick. Follow the instructions on how to cover the board around the cake (page 51).

Make the ice-cream stick

Enlarge the ice-cream stick template (page 189) with a photocopier. Trace on baking paper and cut it out. Roll out the caramel icing to about 1 cm (½ in) thick and mould into the shape of an ice-cream stick, using the template as a guide. Brush a line of water on the correct position on the board and lay the stick over it (step 6).

This is a great cake for beach lovers, surfers or just to celebrate the start of summer. The colours and flowers are easily changed to something more masculine if need be (try fish, suns or stars). Here you'll be introduced to using non-edible materials as decoration, such as the acetate strap.

Flip flop cake

Materials

20 cm (8 in) square cake
100 ml (3½ oz) syrup
1.5 kg (3 lb 5 oz) ganache
1.2 kg (2 lb 10 oz) orange icing (cake and flower centres)
300 g (10½ oz) yellow icing (top layer)
Wooden skewers
100 g (3¾ oz) pink icing (flowers)
Pink royal icing
Clear A4 plastic acetate
Double-sided sticky tape
150 g (5½ oz) royal icing
70 g (2½ oz) raw sugar
Coral brown food colour

Equipment

35 x 50 cm (14 x 20 in) rectangular board (display)
Baking paper
2B pencil
Waxed cardboard (DIY board)
Ganaching tools (page 14)
Serrated knife
Pastry brush
Cranked palette knife
Large and small rolling pins
Plastic scraper
Smoothers
Flexi-scraper
Pizza wheel
Paintbrushes
Wire cutters (secateurs)
Pasta machine
Plastic sheets
Large blossom cutter
Piping bag
No. 2 piping tip

Shape and ganache the flip flop

Enlarge the flip flop template (page 187) with a photocopier. Trace the template onto a sheet of baking paper and cut out, then convert into a DIY board for the cake, using waxed cardboard (page 62).

Follow the instructions (page 40) on how to make a 30 x 20 cm (12 x 8 in) rectangular cake.

Place the flip flop template on top of the cake (step 1, page 149) and use a small serrated knife to cut around it, making sure to hold the knife straight down to maintain a right-angle. Build up the shape of the flip flop with off-cuts sandwiched together with ganache. Smooth the shaped cake with ganache (page 41).

Tip: Focus on the sides of the cake before finishing the top.

Cover the flip flop

Knead 1 kg (2 lb 4 oz) of the orange icing to a pliable dough and roll to 3 mm (⅛ in) thick. Follow the instructions on how to cover a shaped cake (page 47), (step 2).

Apply the top layer

Use a rolling pin to roll the yellow icing to about 3 mm (⅛ in) thick. Place the flip flop template on top and cut around it with a pizza wheel or small knife. Gently lift the icing and place it onto the shaped cake to check the dimensions are correct; the icing should just overlap the sides. If it is not an accurate fit, manipulate the icing by stretching or pushing it.

Using a damp brush, apply a thin layer of syrup all over the cake. With the same brush, gently lift the icing around the sides and brush the base, then stick the icing on the cake with a small amount of syrup.

Prepare the toe area

Insert a wooden skewer into the toe area; leave 4 cm (1½ in) of the skewer above the cake. Clip off the excess with wire cutters or a pair of strong scissors.

Roll out a small piece of orange icing with the pasta machine to about 3 mm (⅛ in) thick. Cut out a small strip of 5 x 2 cm (2 x ¾ in). Wrap the strip around the sides of the skewer and secure with a dab of water (step 3). Mark the position of the straps with a sharp knife about two-thirds of the way down from the top of the flip flop on each side.

Make the flower decoration

Roll out the pink icing and 100 g (3½ oz) of the orange icing in a pasta machine to 3 mm (⅛ in) thick. Using a small flower cutter, cut out flowers in the pink icing and with a no. 2 piping tip cut out the same amount of circles in the orange icing. Stick a

Roughly apply the sand icing with a palette knife around the flip flop on the board to create the beach impression.

circle on the middle of each flower and place the flowers randomly on the flip flop, keeping one flower aside for the strap.

Reknead the icing and roll out again. Using a cutter or a small knife, cut an oval for the label from the orange icing. Fill a piping bag with pink royal icing and with a very small nozzle pipe the name onto the oval shape. Let it dry and then place it onto the flip flop, brushing it with a little water to make it stick.

Make the straps

Cut two acetate strips to the desired width. Stick one end of an acetate strip to the top of the skewer with double-sided sticky tape and push the other end into the marked area (step 4). Use double-sided tape to press a second strip on top of the first one.

Roll out the remaining orange icing in the pasta machine or by hand to 3 mm (⅛ in) thick. Cut four strips the same size as the acetate strips and cover the icing strips with a sheet of plastic.

Brush syrup on the acetate strip and cover it with the icing on both sides (page 60), but leave about 4 cm (1½ in) of the acetate without the icing. Push the uncovered piece of strip into the cake, using the template for the correct position. Repeat this with the other strip. Support the straps with tissue paper until completely dry, then remove (step 5). Stick the remaining flower onto the joining line with a dab of water.

Cover the display board and apply the sand

Follow the instructions on how to cover a board around the cake (page 51), making sure the joining line is at the back of the flip flop. Apply the sand icing onto the board and around the flip flop, using a palette knife. See instructions on how to make the sand (page 61). Decorate the board.

1. Use the template to cut the shape from a rectangular cake.

2. Cover the flip flop in orange icing.

3. Cover the flip flop with yellow icing and mark holes for straps. Insert skewer and trim, then wrap sides with orange icing.

4. Stick acetate strips to the skewer and cover with orange icing.

5. Position flowers and support the straps with tissue paper until dry.

6. Cover the board and decorate with sand icing.

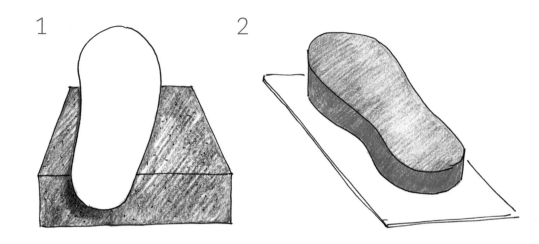

Bake, decorate, blast off! This bold and bright cake will help you perfect your moulding of rounded shapes. The decorations are all created from cut-outs and templates, and you will be painting with edible silver dust to add sparkle.

Rocket cake

Materials
20 cm (8 in) square cake
100 ml (3½ fl oz) syrup
1.2 kg (2 lb 10 oz) ganache
1 kg (2 lb 4 oz) orange icing (cake)
700 g (1 lb 9 oz) black icing (board)
100 g (3½ oz) green icing (door and stars)
50 g (1¾ oz) blue icing (window)
400 g (14 oz) red icing (nose and wings)
50 g (1¾ oz) grey icing (trim and details)
120 g (4¼ oz) yellow icing (strips)
50 g (1¾ oz) black icing (alien)
Edible dust in silver
Decoratoring alcohol
Golden cachous

Equipment
40 cm (16 in) round board (display)
Waxed cardboard (DIY board)
2B pencil
Ganaching tools (page 14)
Serrated knife
Scissors
Large and small rolling pins
Plastic scraper
Smoother
Flexi-scraper
Pizza wheel
Pasta machine
Small knife
Set of circle cutters
Plastic sheets
Paintbrushes
Star cutter
Stitching tool
Frilling tool
No. 1 piping (icing) tip
Clear plastic drinking straw
Cotton wool

Shape and ganache the cake
Enlarge the rocket template (page 188) with a photocopier. Trace the template on baking paper and cut it out. Follow the instructions on how to make a square into a 30 x 20 cm (12 x 8 in) rectangular cake (page 40).

Place the template on top and with a small serrated knife cut out the shape of the rocket (step 1, page 152). Use a serrated knife to taper the front of the rocket to a very low point; keep the top highest part and the middle part about 10–15 cm (4–6 in) high. Use the cake off-cuts to give the rocket its half-round shape, sticking it on with ganache. Keep cutting and sticking till it looks perfectly balanced from every angle. Brush the cake with syrup all over, and then ganache (step 2, page 152). Allow to set.

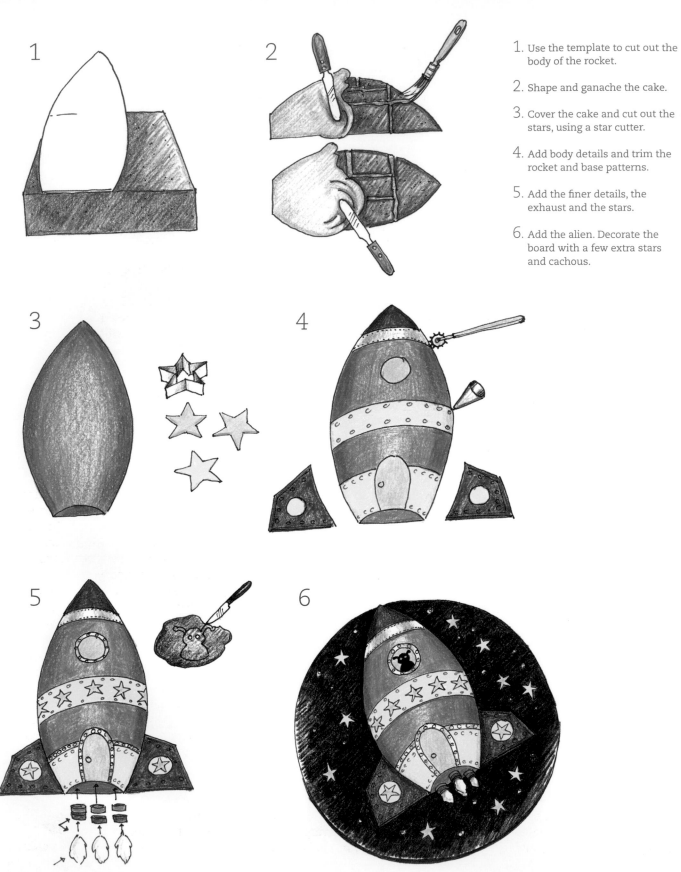

1. Use the template to cut out the body of the rocket.

2. Shape and ganache the cake.

3. Cover the cake and cut out the stars, using a star cutter.

4. Add body details and trim the rocket and base patterns.

5. Add the finer details, the exhaust and the stars.

6. Add the alien. Decorate the board with a few extra stars and cachous.

The smart use of drinking straws and cotton wool creates the effect of smoke coming out of the 'starting' engine.

Create a DIY board

Trace the rocket template you made earlier onto waxed cardboard. Cut it out to make the DIY board to put underneath the cake.

Cover the cake

Knead the orange icing to a pliable dough and roll to 3 mm (⅛ in) thick. Follow the instructions on how to cover a shaped cake (page 47). Keep the edges sharp and trim the icing very neatly at the base (step 3).

Cover the display board

Knead the black icing to a pliable dough and roll to 3 mm (⅛ in) thick. Follow the general instructions on how to cover the board, using either method (page 48).

Make the door and window

Roll out 50 g (1¾ oz) of the green and blue icing to 3 mm (⅛ in) thick. Using the template, cut out the door and use a medium circle cutter to cut out the window. Cover the shapes with plastic to prevent drying out.

Make the trims and details

For the nose, roll out 20 g (¾ oz) of the red icing to 3 mm (⅛ in) thick. Brush the nose area with a little water and place the red icing over it, making sure to align it properly. Cut away the excess icing with a knife.

For the strips, roll out about 80 g (2¾ oz) of the yellow icing and 40 g (1½ oz) of the grey icing to 3 mm (⅛ in) thick. Cut two yellow strips and one grey strip of 3 cm (1¼ in) wide and long enough to cover the rocket from side to side. Brush the rocket with a little water and stick on the strips. Place the door template on the bottom strip and cut out a gap. Stick the door and the window on the rocket with a dab of water (steps 3+4).

For the stars, roll out the remaining green icing and the remaining yellow icing to 3 mm (⅛ in) thick and cut out 17 stars using a star cutter (step 3). Stick them onto the rocket and board with a dab of water. Save two stars for the wings.

For the silver trims, roll out the remaining grey icing to 3 mm (⅛ in) thick. Using a circle cutter, cut out a circle and with a smaller circle cutter cut away the inner circle. Stick this over the window to get the window frame. For the door, roll a very thin grey sausage. Dampen the edge of the door and stick the thin sausage around the door. Use a stitching tool, piping tip and frilling tool to create effects (step 4). Mix the silver dust with decorating alcohol and paint the grey icing (page 61). Allow to dry.

Make the finishing touches

For the wings, roll out the remaining red icing to about 5 mm (¼ in) thick. Use the template to cut out the wings with a pizza wheel or a small knife. Stick the wings on the board right next to the rocket with a little bit of water.

For the engines, roll a small amount of leftover orange icing (about the size of a hazelnut) into a ball, then mould it to a disc between your index finger and thumb. Do the same with the leftover red icing but make the disc a bit smaller. Repeat to make three of each. Stick the orange discs on the red discs (step 5). Brush the end of the rocket with a little water and stick the engines, orange side down, on it (step 6).

For the smoke, cut an extra large clear drinking straw into three 5 cm (2 in) long pieces. Poke a little cotton wool in the end of the straw. Repeat this with the other two straws. Stick the straws into the engines so that only the smoke is seen.

For the alien, roll the black icing to 3 mm (⅛ in) thick. Trace an alien DIY template onto baking paper and cut it out. Place the template on the black icing and cut around it with a small knife (step 5). Stick your alien character on the window with a dab of water (step 6).

Stick the cachous around the rocket on the bord with a litle water.

Perfect for any fashionistas you know. Once you've mastered the boot you can change the shape to make any shoe you like. This cake introduces you to hand painting and is a great opportunity to let your imagination run wild.

Boot cake

Materials
20 cm (8 in) square cake
1.5 kg (3 lb 5 oz) ganache
100 ml (3½ fl oz) syrup
1.5 kg (3 lb 5 oz) ivory icing (cake)
500 g (1 lb 2 oz) caramel icing (sole and heel)
Black and brown food colouring
Decorating alcohol
400 g (14 oz) orange icing (bow)

Equipment
30 x 50 cm (12 x 20 in) rectangular board (display)
Large and small rolling pins
Plastic scraper
Smoothers
Flexi-scraper
Baking paper
2B pencil
Ganaching tools (page 14)
Serrated knife
Pastry brush
Cranked palette knife
Small sharp kitchen knife
Plastic sheets
Paintbrushes
Pasta machine

Cover the display board
Follow the instructions on how to cover the whole board (page 49). Allow to dry and harden. (You will be placing the semi-finished cake onto the board.)

Shape the cake
Follow the instructions on how to cut the cake into a 30 x 20 cm (12 x 8 in) rectangular shape (page 40). Enlarge the boot template (page 186) with a photocopier. Trace the template onto baking paper and cut out. Once the cake is joined and filled, place the template on top and cut around it. Use the off-cuts to build the shape (step 2, page 156). Smooth the ganache and let set.

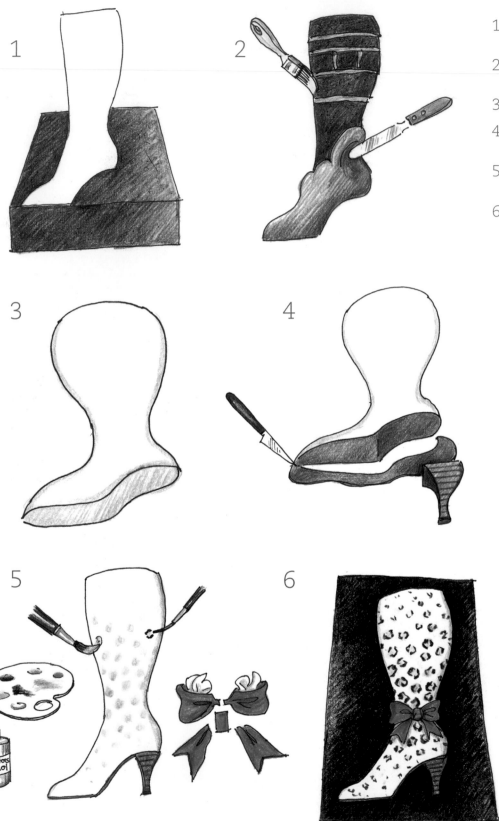

1. Use the template to cut the boot from the cake.

2. Bind the cake with syrup and cover with ganache.

3. Cover the cake.

4. Apply the sole and make the high heel.

5. Paint the pattern on the boot and make the bow.

6. Place the bow around the ankle of the boot.

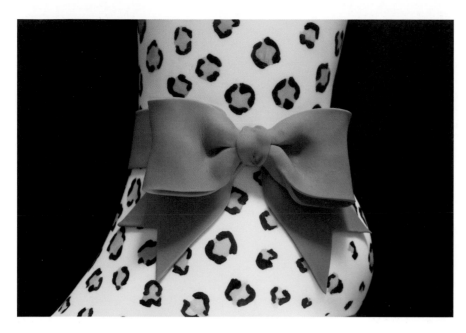

The striking colour of the bow adds a great contrast to the animal print.

Cover the cake
Measure the boot and brush lightly with syrup. Knead the ivory icing to a pliable dough, roll out to 3 mm (⅛ in) thick. Cover the cake with the icing (step 3), following the instructions on how to cover a shaped cake (page 47).

Apply the sole and make the heel
Knead 300 g (10½ oz) of the caramel icing to a pliable consistency and roll to 3 mm (⅛ in) thick. Roughly cut the icing in the shape of the sole and stick underneath the boot. Using a sharp small knife trim the edges. Mould a heel out of the remaining caramel icing. Measure the distance between the sole and where it will sit to find the right height for the heel. Using your fingers to create a cone first, then mould it into the shape of a heel. Use the back of a knife to decorate the heel. Let it dry, then stick it onto the board underneath the sole with a dab of water (step 4).

Paint the pattern
Combine the brown food colour with the decorating alcohol. Paint the brown spots in random size and pattern onto the boot, starting from the centre and working to the sides and up and down.

Combine the black food colouring with the cake decorating alcohol and paint around the brown spots to create an animal skin pattern (step 5). Work quickly, as your paints will dry out fast (page 61).

Make the bow
Knead 350 g (12 oz) of the orange icing to a pliable dough. Follow the instructions on how to make a bow (page 58).

Place the bow
Roll out the remaining orange icing to 3 mm (⅛ in) thick.

For the anklet ribbon cut a strip of icing to 15 x 2 cm (6 x ¾ in), and place it onto the boot around the ankle with a thin line of water. Trim the excess strip.

For the ribbon 'tails', cut two fat rectangles in the same width as your bow and about 5 cm (2 in) long. Cut a V shape out of one end of each tail and place it underneath the bow. Place the semi-dry bow on top and stick with a dab of water (steps 5+6). Allow to dry.

Tip: For a puffy bow, place some tissue paper or cotton wool in the loops and remove when the icing has dried.

Three-dimensional cakes

We do, of course, know that all cakes are three-dimensional, but this is what we call our spectacular sculpted, modelled creations. They're fun, fantastic, and obviously a bit more tricky to make (which is why they're at the end of the book). Don't be nervous — you have all the techniques perfected by now.

You've got the skills now, so reach for the sky. This cake is a great introduction to sculpting. The aeroplane is cartoonish rather than realistic, so keep everything rounded and child-like.

Aeroplane cake

Material
20 cm (8 in) square cake
100 ml (3½ fl oz) syrup
1.5 kg (3 lb 5 oz) ganache
1.1 kg (2 lb 7 oz) white icing (cake and clouds)
1 kg (2 lb 4 oz) sky blue icing (board)
100 g (3½ oz) black icing (strips and eyes)
50 g (1¾ oz) grey icing (nose)
300 g (10½ oz) light blue icing (wings and rudder)
100 g (3½ oz) watermelon coloured icing (strips)
2 toothpicks
Decorating alcohol
Black food colour

Equipment
46 cm (18 in) round board (display)
2B pencil
Waxed cardboard (DIY board)
Ganaching tools (page 14)
Serrated knife
Pastry brush
Cranked palette knife
Large and small rolling pins
Plastic scraper
Smoother
Flexi-scraper
Pasta machine
Plastic sheet
Frilling tool
Paintbrushes
Set of circle cutters

Prepare and shape the cake
Enlarge the aeroplane template (page 186) with a photocopier. Trace the template onto a sheet of waxed cardboard and cut it out. Follow the instructions on how to make a square into a rectangular cake (page 40). Then read the instructions on how to ganache a shaped cake (page 41). Once the cake is filled, place the template on top and cut around it (step 1, page 162). Use the off-cuts to build the front of the aeroplane (step 2). The front part is almost as rounded as a ball. Taper the tail part downwards. Ganache the cake and place it on the final board (step 2, page 162). Let set.

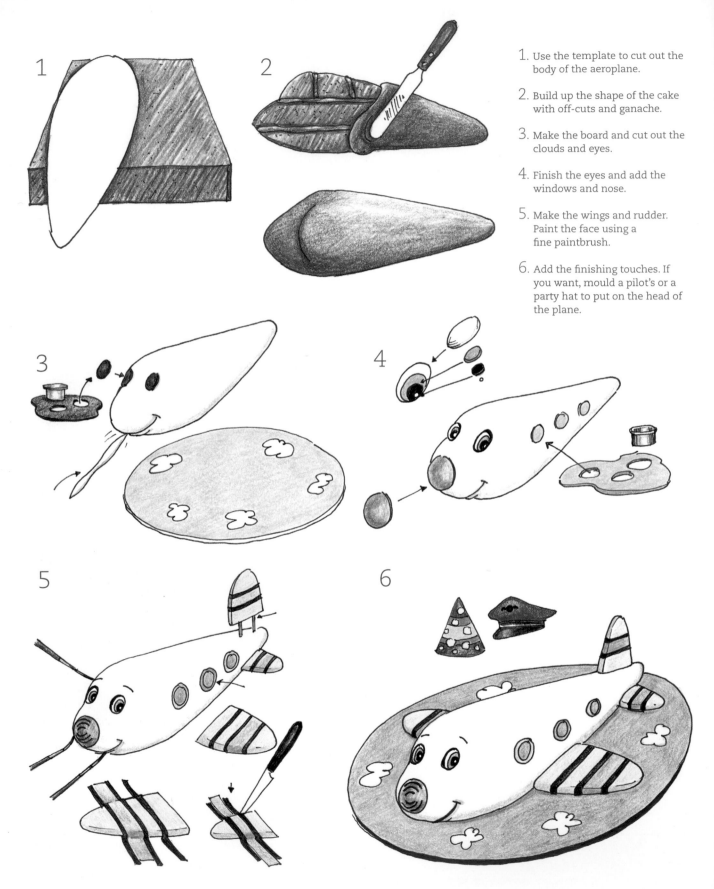

1. Use the template to cut out the body of the aeroplane.

2. Build up the shape of the cake with off-cuts and ganache.

3. Make the board and cut out the clouds and eyes.

4. Finish the eyes and add the windows and nose.

5. Make the wings and rudder. Paint the face using a fine paintbrush.

6. Add the finishing touches. If you want, mould a pilot's or a party hat to put on the head of the plane.

Wrap strips in different colours and widths around the wings to create a cartoonish look.

Cover the cake
Knead 1 kg (2 lb 4 oz) of the white icing to a pliable dough and roll to 3 mm (⅛ in) thick. Follow the instructions on how to cover a shaped cake (page 47).

Cover the display board
Knead 800 g (1 lb 12 oz) of the sky blue icing to a pliable dough and roll to 3 mm (⅛ in) thick. Follow the instructions on how to cover a board around the cake (page 51).

Make the clouds
Draw your own cloud templates in two different sizes. Roll the remaining white icing to 3 mm (⅛ in) thick. Place the template on top and cut around it. Stick the clouds on the board with a little water (step 3).

Make the face
For the mouth and eyes, while the icing is still soft use a frilling tool to indent the mouth at the front of the plane (step 3). Press your thumb into the cake to indent the eyes.
Roll out small amounts of black, sky blue and leftover white icing to

3 mm (⅛ in) thick and cover it with plastic. Cut out two black 2 x 1 cm (1 x ½ in) ovals, using either a round cutter and then stretching the circles slightly or by cutting free hand. Cut out two smaller white ovals and blue ovals and even smaller ovals in black (step 4). Finish with two tiny white ovals. With a little water stick the ovals on the cake, starting with a large black oval followed by white, blue, black and white ovals reducing in size.

For the nose, roll out the grey icing to 3 mm (⅛ in) thick. Cut out a disc using a 5 cm (2 in) circle cutter. Stick the nose on the cake with a little water (step 4).

Make the windows
Use a 3 cm (1¼ in) circle cutter to indent three windows on each side of the plane. Roll out some of the sky blue icing to 3 mm (⅛ in) and using the circle cutter, cut out six discs for the windows. Stick three windows on each side of the plane with a little water (step 4). Make two long thin rolls from the light blue icing and the watermelon icing. Cut into six lengths long enough to go around

the windows and stick them on with a little water (step 5).

Make the wings and rudder
Roll out the remaining light blue icing to 1.5 cm (5/8 in) thick and, with a small sharp knife, cut out the four wings and rudder using the template (page 186). Smooth the outer edges of the pieces with your fingers, but not where they join the plane. Roll out the remaining black and watermelon coloured icing to 3 mm (⅛ in) thick. Using a pizza wheel or a small sharp knife, cut out strips in different widths long enough to cover the wings. Stick them on the wings with a little water and trim (step 5). Stick wings on the board next to the plane with a little water (step 5). Poke two toothpicks into the rudder from underneath, at the joining edge. Stick the rudder on the aeroplane with a little water (step 5).

Paint the face
Mix black food colour and a drop of decorating alcohol. Paint the eyebrows, mouth and details on the nose (step 5).

Every time we create a 'food' cake at Planet Cake, people respond with rapturous applause and child-like wonder. You'll need an especially firm cake here, such as the chocolate mud cake. Modelling the icing is one of the most enjoyable cake-decorating skills to master.

Barbecue cake

Materials
22 cm (9 in) round cake
100 ml (3½ fl oz) syrup
1.5 kg (3 lb 5 oz) ganache
30 g (1 oz) black icing (coal)
200 g (7 oz) grey icing (coal)
50 g (1¾ oz) orange icing (flame)
50 g (1¾ oz) black icing (flame)
50 g (1¾ oz) red icing (flame)
1 kg (2 lb 4 oz) red icing (cake)
700 g (1 lb 9 oz) green icing (board)
100 g (3½ oz) black royal icing
100 g (3½ oz) caramel icing (handle)
Black, caramel, yellow, brown, red & blue food colours
300 g (10½ oz) white icing (meat)
20 g (¾ oz) green icing (capsicum)
20 g (¾ oz) red icing (capsicum)
8 toothpicks
Edible silver dust
Decorating alcohol
Glaze

Equipment
22 cm (9 in) round board (set-up)
13 cm (5 in) round board (set-up)
35 cm (14 in) round board (display)
Ganaching tools (page 14)
Serrated knife
Pastry brush
Cranked palette knife
Large and small rolling pins
Plastic scraper
Smoother
Flexi-scraper
Pizza wheel
Pasta machine
Plastic sheet
Ruler
Frilling tool
Paring knife
Paintbrush
Piping bag
No. 3 piping tip
Kitchen scourer

Prepare and shape the cake
Follow the instructions on how to prepare and ganache a round cake (page 38), but only fill the layers. Once it is filled, start shaping the cake by placing it on a turntable with the 22 cm (9 in) board on the bottom and the 13 cm (5 in) board on the top as a guide for tapering. Stick the off-cuts to the cake with ganache to build up the inverted bowl shape. Keep in mind as you are shaping the cake that it is upside down (step 1, page 166).

Turn the cake, roughly ganache and let set, preferably overnight (step 2, page 166).

Make the coal
Partially mix some black icing into the grey icing to give it a streaky effect (page 61). Roll out the grey

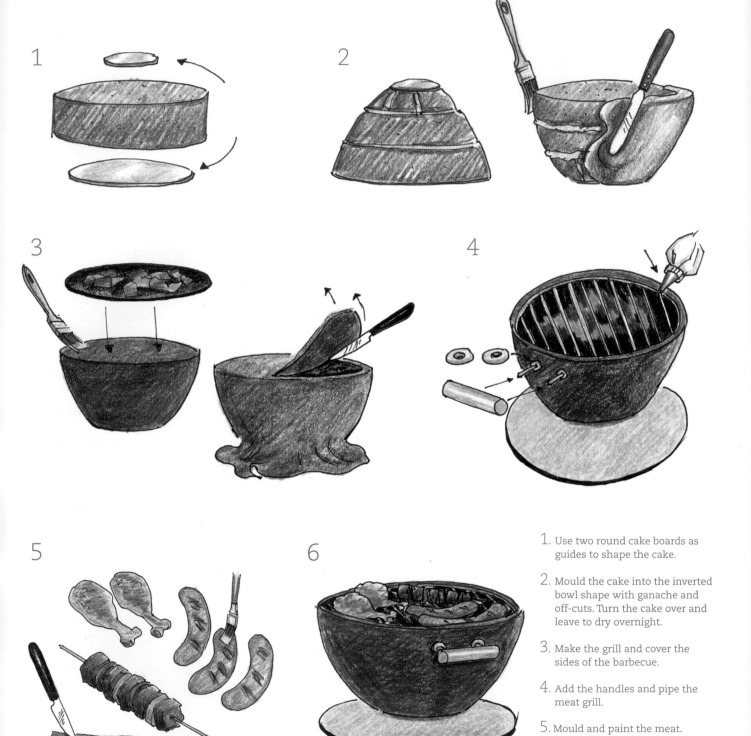

1. Use two round cake boards as guides to shape the cake.

2. Mould the cake into the inverted bowl shape with ganache and off-cuts. Turn the cake over and leave to dry overnight.

3. Make the grill and cover the sides of the barbecue.

4. Add the handles and pipe the meat grill.

5. Mould and paint the meat.

6. Assemble the barbecue and add the finishing touches.

To get the barbecued effect for the meat, mark charred lines with the back of a knife and paint the lines with brown food colour.

icing to 5 cm (¼ in) thick and large enough to cover the top of the cake. Place pieces of orange, black and red icing randomly on the grey icing. Roll out again with the sprinkled pieces on top to about 3 mm (⅛ in) thick. Using a 22 cm (9 in) cake board as a template, cut the icing with a pizza wheel. Brush the top of the cake with syrup and place the icing on top. Manipulate the icing to fit (step 3). Let dry.

For the grill, use a ruler to mark the lines every 2 cm (¾ in), and create the grooves with a frilling tool or the back of a paring knife.

Cover the cake

Brush the side of the cake (not the top) with syrup. Measure the height and circumference of the cake and roll out the red icing to 3 mm (⅛ in) thick. Cover the cake, following the instructions on how to cover a shaped cake (page 47). Press the icing against the side (step 3). Put the 22 cm (9 in) cake board on top of the cake and cut around the board, making sure not to damage the charcoal base. Lift the red icing up, smooth the edges with the flexi-scraper and trim at the base. Push the icing inwards with a frilling tool.

Cover the display board

Roll out the green icing to 3 mm (⅛ in) thick and follow the instructions on how to cover the board (page 48), using either method. While the icing is still soft press a kitchen scourer in the icing to create a grass texture.

Make the grill

Fill a piping bag with black royal icing. With a no. 3 piping tip, pipe along the grooves on the grill top (step 4). Mix edible silver dust with decorating alcohol and paint the grill.

Tip: If you are not confident with piping, roll thin black sausages and place them along the grooves with a dab of water and paint when dry.

Make the handles

Roll out 80 g (2¾ oz) of the caramel icing and cut two rectangles about 1 cm (½ in) thick, 8 cm (3¼ in) long and 2 cm (¾ in) wide. In addition, make four small round 1 cm (½ in) thick discs. When the handles are semi-dry, poke two toothpicks into each side of the cake and skewer one disc on each toothpick using royal icing as glue. Stack the handles on top of the toothpicks and discs (step 4).

Make the meat and the kebab

To make the kebab meat, mix a little yellow, brown and blue food colour into white icing and roll into a long brick shape. Cut into slices using a paring knife in a sawing motion to get a meat effect. Use a paintbrush to lightly paint the pieces with brown food colour mixed with decorating alcohol to exaggerate the colour.

For the capsicums, roll out the green and red icings to about 2 mm (1⁄16 in) thick. Cut into squares, then curl slightly for a natural look. Use a bit of brown food colour mixed with decorating alcohol and paint marks on the edges for a barbecued effect.

When partially dry, place the meat and capsicum pieces together to look like a kebab and poke toothpicks in the end to imitate skewers (step 5, see **Note** page 11).

For the chicken drumsticks, add drops of brown and yellow food colour to the white icing and roll into a ball. Mould into a large teardrop then shape into a drumstick. Add skin texture with a grater. Mark charred lines with the back of a paring knife and paint the lines brown with undiluted food colour. Partially paint the leg with brown food colour mixed with alcohol to give it a cooked effect.

For the sausage, mix brown and red into the white icing, then mould into two balls and roll into sausages. Bend slightly. Mark charred lines with the back of a paring knife and paint them with undiluted brown food colour. Mix brown and red food colour with decorating alcohol and brush the sausages.

Assemble the barbecue

Stick the kebabs on top of the barbecue with royal icing then add the drumsticks and sausages. Follow the instructions on how to glaze (page 54). Glaze the meat on the barbecue (step 5).

This stunning cake is always the star of any party. While the giant cupcake looks incredibly professional, the majority of energy is required for perfecting the dome shape rather than decorating.

Giant cupcake

Material

20 cm (8 in) square cake
100 ml (3½ fl oz) syrup
1.5 kg (3 lb 5 oz) ganache
100 g (3½ oz) white icing (separator)
3 wooden skewers
450 g (1 lb) brown icing (cake)
300 g (10½ oz) blue icing ('paper case')
300 g (10½ oz) white icing (icing)
100 g (3½ oz) red royal icing (sprinkles)
100 g (3½ oz) blue royal icing (sprinkles)
40 g (1½ oz) red icing (cherry)
700 g ((1 lb 9 oz) white icing (board)
Glaze
Green florist tape

Equipment

Ganaching tools (page 14)
13 cm (5 in) round board (set-up)
18 cm (7 in) round board (set-up)
35 cm (14 in) round board (display)
Large and small rolling pins
Plastic scraper
Cranked palette knife
Smoother
Large serrated knife
Flexi-scraper
Pastry brush
Paintbrush
Frilling tool
No. 2 piping tip
Piping bag
Pizza wheel
Pasta machine
Small wire covered with green
Florist tape
Baking paper

Prepare and shape the cake

For the base, cut the cake in three even layers and sandwich them together with ganache. Follow the instructions on how to prepare and ganache (pages 38–39). Centre the 13 cm (5 in) round cake board on top and the 18 cm (7 in) round board underneath the square cake, using a dab of ganache to hold them in place (step 1, page 170). Keep in mind as you are working that the cake is upside down.

Use a large serrated knife to taper the cake out towards the base, and a small serrated knife to shave the cake until it looks neat and the top of the cake is 18 cm (7 in). Turn the cake right side up (step 2, page 170).

Push in the three wooden skewers within the 13 cm (5 in) diameter and trim flush with the cake (step 3).

1. Use the different-sized round boards as guides to shape the base of the cupcake.

2. Invert the cake and shape the dome.

3. Use wooden skewers and ganache to shape the dome.

4. Cover the dome with chocolate icing and trim flush with the base. Cover the base and use a wooden skewer to make the 'paper case' decorations.

5. Ice the dome and pipe on the coloured sprinkles. Make the cherry and glaze.

6. Add the finishing touches.

Devote a bit of time making the cherry to achieve the most realistic shape. The glaze gives the cherry a beautiful glossy finish.

Make the separator and dome

Roll the white icing to 2 mm (1/16 in) thick using the 18 cm (7 in) cake board as a template, and cut it out with a pizza wheel. With a dab of ganache, stick the icing on top of the layered cake and stick the cake board on top of the icing.

Build the dome with the off-cuts, using ganache for sticking it on. Keep shaving the dome unil it looks perfectly balanced from every angle (page 41). Stick your cake on the 13 cm (5 in) set-up board, ganache and let set.

Cover the cake

Follow the instructions on how to cover a shaped cake (page 47). Measure the circumference and the height of the cake from the top to just below the dome. Brush the area of the dome that will be covered with icing with water or syrup.

Knead the brown icing to a pliable dough and roll out to about 3 mm (1/8 in) thick.

Cover the dome and smooth with the flexi-scraper. Trim the icing just below the dome (step 4).

For the 'paper case', measure the circumference and height of the base. Roll out the blue icing to about 3 mm (1/8 in) thick and large enough to cover the base. Cut into a rectangle. Brush the cake with syrup and wrap the icing around the cake (page 47). Mark the 'paper case' indentations with a barbecue skewer (page 62). For the icing on the dome, enlarge the template (page 187) with a photocopier. Trace it on baking paper and cut it out. Measure the area to be covered and brush with syrup. Roll the white icing to 3 mm (1/8 in) thick. Put your template on top of the icing and cut it out (step 5). Stick the icing on top of the dome.

Make the sprinkles

Fill a piping bag one-third full with the red royal icing. Using a no. 2 piping tip, pipe sprinkles over the dome of the cake. Clean the piping bag and fill with the blue royal icing, then pipe sprinkles over the dome.

Make the cherry

Roll the red icing into a smooth ball and taper slightly on one side. Make an indent in the top with the frilling tool. Insert twisted green florist tape for the stalk and bend slightly; use a toothpick if required (step 5). Follow the instructions on how to glaze (page 54). Glaze the cherry.

Cover the display board

Knead the white icing to a pliable dough. Follow the instructions on how to cover a board (page 49). Stick the cake on the board with royal icing.

171

It's a great idea to have a real tube of paint (or even toothpaste!) in front of you while you make this. Modelling and sculpting are always easier if you have something to copy from.

Paint tube cake

Materials
20 cm (8 in) square cake
100 ml (3½ fl oz) syrup
1.5 kg (3 lb 5 oz) ganache
1.3 kg (3 lb) white icing (cake)
100 g (3½ oz) orange icing (tube)
200 g (7 oz) blue icing (tube)
50 g (1¾ oz) white icing (nozzle)
100 g (3½ oz) red icing (lid)
50 g (1¾ oz) white icing (label)
50 g (1¾ oz) red icing (letters)
1 kg (2 lb 4 oz) white icing (board)
Edible silver dust
Decorating alcohol
Glaze
100 g (3½ oz) red royal icing
100 g (3½ oz) white royal icing
2 toothpicks

Equipment
Ganaching tools (page 14)
60 x 40 cm (24 x 16 in) rectangular
    board (display)
30 x 20 cm (12 x 8 in) rectangular
    board (set-up)
Large and small rolling pins
Plastic scraper
Cranked palette knife
Smoother
Serrated knife
Flexi-scraper
Flexible ruler
Pastry brush
Paintbrushes
Frilling tool
Piping bag
No. 8 piping tip
Alphabet cutters (or DIY template)
Set of circle cutters
Pasta machine
Waxed cardboard (DIY board)
2B pencil

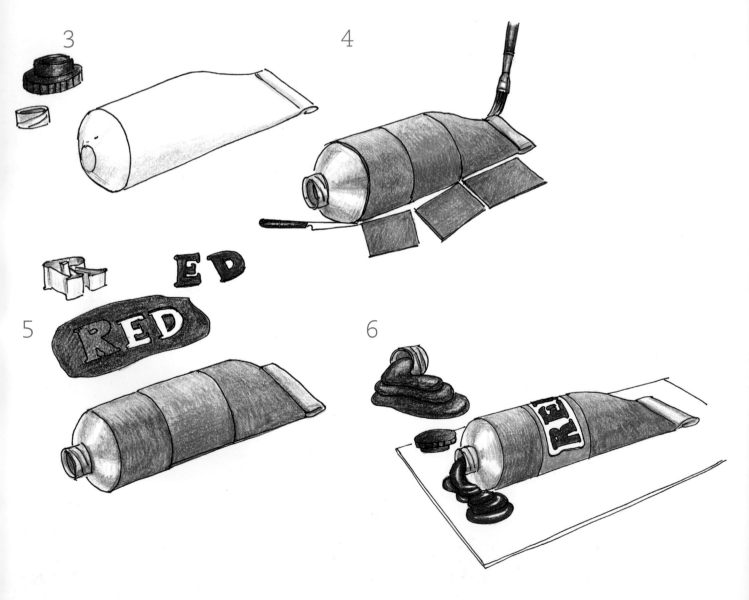

1. Prepare the cake.

2. Shape and ganache the cake.

3. Cover the tube, nozzle and lid.

4. Make the tube colours.

5. Make the label and name stencils for the tag.

6. Pipe the oozing paint and assemble the cake.

With a set of alphabet cutters you can create any word you like. For a longer word, stick the label lengthways down the paint tube.

Prepare the cake

The paint tube requires as much height as possible. Therefore, cut one 5 cm (2 in) slice off the square and ganache it on the cake to make a 15 x 25 cm (6 x 10 in) rectangle. Enlarge the template (page 188), trace on baking paper and cut it out. Place the template on top of the cake and with a large serrated knife, start cutting the long side of the cake to create a three-quarter round cylinder (use a real tube to copy the shape). Use the cake off-cuts to add more height where needed, sticked together with ganache.

Taper the end of the tube until it is very flat (step 2).

Cut the cylinder at the top into a dome shape (step 2). Continue cutting until the paint tube looks good from every angle.

Taper the cake at the base. Roughly ganache and let set, then hot-knife the cake following the instructions on how to ganache a cake (page 38).

Make a DIY board

Trace the paint tube template on waxed cardboard and cut out to get a DIY board (page 62). Place the cake on the board.

Cover the cake

Knead the white icing into a pliable dough and roll to 3 mm (⅛ in) thick. Follow the instructions on how to cover a shaped cake (page 47).

Unroll the icing at the base of the tube. Keep the rounded edge at the front smooth by using two flexi-scrapers and trim the icing very neatly at the base. Use a flexible plastic ruler to push the icing in at the base. Cut the back of the tube straight. Mark indents in the icing to give it a rolled-up effect (step 3).

Make the nozzle and lid

For the nozzle, knead the white icing to a pliable dough and roll into a cylinder 6 cm (2½ in) in diameter and 2 cm (¾ in) thick. With the back of a knife, mark about five lines all

Pipe layers of oozing paint to create the effect of paint coming out of the tube.

around the cylinder like a nozzle thread. Keep flat until dry.

For the lid, knead the red icing to a pliable dough and roll out to 2 cm (¾ in) thick. Cut a circle using a 6 cm (2½ in) circle cutter. Roll out another small piece of red icing to about 1.5 cm (⅝ in) thick and cut with a large circle cutter (about 10 cm/4 in). Stick to the top of the smaller red disc with a dab of water and mark indentations around the side with a frilling tool. Keep flat until dry.

Make the tube colours

Roll the orange and blue icing to 3 mm (⅛ in) thick. With a ruler and a pizza wheel cut three 12 cm (4½ in) wide strips, long enough to be wraped around the tube.

Brush water onto each designated area of the tube and place each strip on it, making sure to keep it straight. Brush a thin line of water in between the strips so they also join together. Smooth over with a flexi-scraper (step 4, page 174).

Make the label

Roll the red icing in a pasta machine or by hand to 3 mm (⅛ in) thick. Dust your work surface with a little cornflour and place the icing on top. Let the icing dry slightly. Cut out the letters using alphabet cutters. Roll the white icing to 3 mm (⅛ in) thick and cut it into the length and width required for letters.

Stick the letters on the label with a dab of water (step 5, page 174).

Cover the display board

Knead the white icing to a pliable dough and roll out to 3 mm (⅛ in) thick and follow the instructions on how to cover the board (page 48), using either method.

Place the nozzle

Remember that the tube is not a complete circle, so do not place the nozzle in the centre. Stick the nozzle on with royal icing. Mix the edible silver dust with decorating alcohol and paint the front and the back of the tube.

Tip: If the weather is humid the nozzle may not stick. In this case you can use toothpicks. Make a hole at the end of the nozzle with the frilling tool and stick two toothpicks through: when it is dry fasten the nozzle to the tube with the toothpicks. The toothpicks will stay in the cake so make sure to warn everyone who will eat from the cake.

Make the oozing paint

Fill a piping bag fitted with a no. 8 piping tip with the red royal icing. Pipe the ooze, making sure to finish near the paint nozzle. Lift the icing up to the nozzle to create the effect of paint coming out of the tube. Alternatively, you can roll red icing and mould it for the same effect.

The handbag is one of the most popular cake designs at Planet Cake. You can easily personalise the monogram and colours or incorporate the signature details of a favourite designer. Practise your quilting on a spare bit of icing before you work on the real cake.

Handbag cake

Materials
20 cm (8 in) square cake
100 ml (3½ fl oz) syrup
1.5 kg (3 lb 5 oz) ganache
1.5 kg (3 lb 5 oz) pink icing (cake)
Wooden dowel
2 x 30 cm (12 in) lengths 1 cm (½ in)
   diameter plastic aquarium tubing
Toothpicks
Piping gel
500 g (1 lb 2 oz) black icing (handles
   & decoration)
Edible gold dust
Decorating alcohol
700 g (1 lb 9 oz) white icing (board)

Equipment
Ganaching tools (page 14)
35 cm (14 in) round board
30 x 20 cm (12 x 8 in) rectangular
   board
Large and small rolling pins
Plastic scraper
Cranked palette knife
Smoother
Serrated knife
Flexi-scraper
Plastic sheets
Serrated dough wheel
Stitching tool
Pastry brush
Medium paintbrush
Frilling tool
45° triangular ruler
Waxed cardboard (DIY template)
No. 4 piping tip
Baking paper
2B pencil
Scissors
Pin
Pasta machine

Use your stitching tool to mark the quilting. To personalise the handbag, stick the birthday girl's initials or a favourite monogram over the quilting.

Shape and ganache the cake

Enlarge the template (page 188) with a photocopier. Trace the template for the top on baking paper and the template for the base on waxed cardboard. Cut them out and use the waxed cardboard template as a DIY board to put underneath the cake.

Cut your square cake into three equal bricks. Ganache the three parts on top of each other, and taper the sides and build up the handbag shape with the off-cuts. Follow the instructions on how to shape a three-dimensional cake (page 41).

Once you have the required shape, ganache the whole cake. Follow the instructions on how to ganache a cake (page 38). Allow the ganache to set (step 1).

Cover the cake

Knead the pink icing to a pliable dough and roll out to 3 mm (⅛ in) thick. Cover the cake, pinching at the sides and trimming away the excess with a small sharp knife and scissors. Smooth the cake and trim the icing at the base and edges (step 2).

Mark the quilting

While the icing is still soft and starting from the left side crease, use a pin to mark the icing every 4 cm (1½ in) along the base (the last section may not be the exact size, but that is all right). Repeat on the other side (the back) of the cake.

Using the triangular ruler and starting from the left side, place the short side on the board at the first pin mark and glide the back of your paring knife along the edge of the triangle to mark a line to the top of the cake. Repeat at each pin mark.

Once all the lines are marked, repeat the same method starting at the right side (step 3) to create the quilting effect. Run the stitching tool along the lines to create the stitching marks (step 3).

Make the handles

Cut four lengths of wooden dowels thick enough to fit snugly into the ends of the plastic tubing (if too thin use toothpicks as fillers) to 10 cm (4 in) long. Push 2.5 cm (1 in) of the dowel into both ends of the tubes. Sharpen the other ends of the dowel

with a pencil sharpener and poke them into a piece of styrofoam 15 cm (6 in) apart (step 4). Brush the tubes with piping gel.

Roll out 300 g (10½ oz) of the black icing to about 3 mm (⅛ in) thick and cut a strip 30 cm (12 in) long and 4 cm (1½ in) wide. Cover the strips with plastic to prevent from drying out. Stick the strips around the tubes with piping gel, using your fingers to smooth the icing. Trim away any excess with scissors or a knife and smooth with your fingers or a flexi-scraper. Leave to dry.

Note: Since your are using plastic tubes as a base for the handles, the handles won't be edible. Therefore, make sure not to serve them.

Make the zipper

Roll out 20 g (¾ oz) of the leftover pink icing to 3 mm (⅛ in) thick. Cut two strips as long as the top of the handbag, one 2.5 cm (1 in) wide and the other 6 mm (¼ in) wide. Cover the wider strip with plastic. Run a serrated dough wheel along the thin strip to mark a zipper line (page 60).

1 2 3 4 5 6

1. Shape and ganache the cake.

2. Cover the cake.

3. Mark the quilted pattern on the sides of the handbag.

4. Make the handles.

5. Make the zipper, the decorative triangle and the monogram.

6. Assemble the cake.

Paint the zipper with gold dust mixed with decorating alcohol to create a metallic look.

Use a ruler and stitching tool to mark a line on both edges of the wider strip. Stick the thinner strip on top of the wider strip and stick the zipper on the handbag with a little water. Trim any excess.

Roll a small pink icing ball to the size of a pea and mould it into a rectangle lightly tapered to one side. Stick it on top of the zipper.

Make the tongue of the zipper the same way, without tapering the rectangle. Cut out a hole with the no. 4 piping tip and let it dry. Stick it on the tapered rectangle (step 5, page 181). Mix the edible gold dust with decorating alcohol and brush it over the zipper using a paintbrush.

Place the handles
To make sure the handles are positioned in the centre of the handbag, measure the zipper to find its centre and then measure 7.5 cm (3 in) to either side of the centre. Mark the icing with a pin. Stick the wooden dowels into the holes.

Remember that the cake is tapered. If you poke the dowel straight down you might pierce the side of the cake and make a hole. Repeat with the other handle.Make four rolls of black icing about 1 cm (½ in) thick and about 20 cm (8 in) long. Knot them around the base of the handles.

Make the monogram and triangle
For the triangle, roll out 50 g (1¾ oz) of the black icing to about 3 mm (⅛ in) thick. Using the template (page 188) cut out the side-trim triangle. Brush some water on the cake and stick the triangle on, trim the edges and smooth either with your finger or the flexi-scraper (step 5, page 181).

For the monogram, use the template in this book (page 188) or any you like and enlarge it to the size you want. Roll out black icing to about 3 mm (⅛ in) thick. Cut the letters from the icing with a small knife and stick them on the cake with a dab of water (step 5).

Cover the display board
Enlarge the template for the base (page 188) with a photocopier, trace on baking paper and cut it out. Follow the instructions on how to cover the board around the cake (page 51). Roll out the white icing to 3 mm (⅛ in) thick and about 5 cm (2 in) larger than the size of the board. Put the template on the icing and cut around it, then take the centre piece out.

Cut a slit in the remaining icing to allow access for the cake. As you where fitting a horseshoe, place the icing on the board around the cake making sure the slit is at the back. Ensure the icing meets perfectly at the back, overlap the icing and re-cut the slit (page 51).

Dampen the board with water or syrup to make the icing stick to the board, then smooth the icing with the flexi-scraper. Use an acrylic smoother or flexi-scraper to trim the icing at the end of the board.

Templates

All the templates you need for the cakes appear in this section. Each template is marked with the percentage of enlargement required to create the correct size with a photocopier.

Princess cake
page 104
Enlarge by 166%

Make-up box cake
Indentation stencil for the make-up box
page 132
Enlarge by 166%

Boot cake
page 154
Enlarge by 200%

Aeroplane cake
page 160
Enlarge by 200%

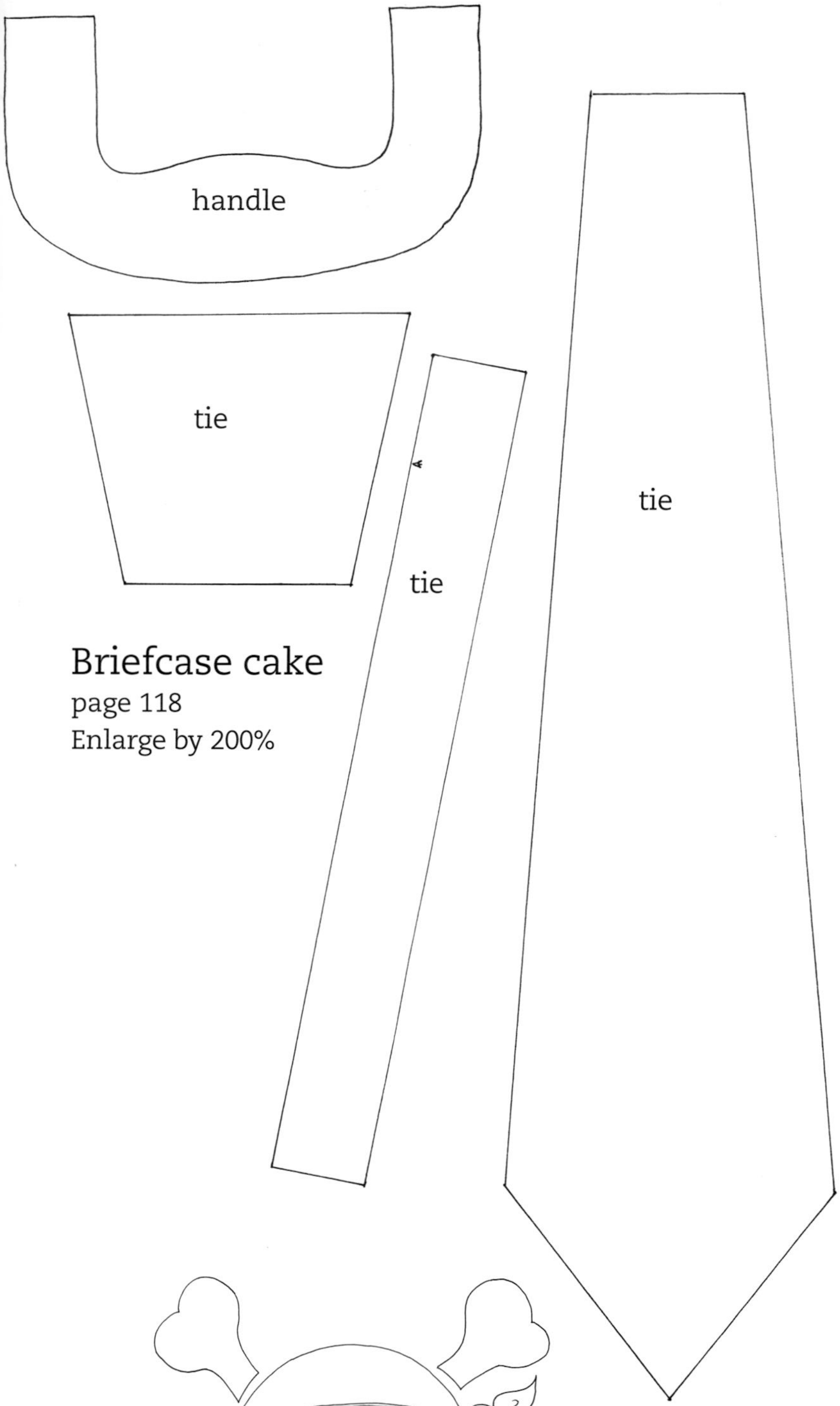

handle

tie

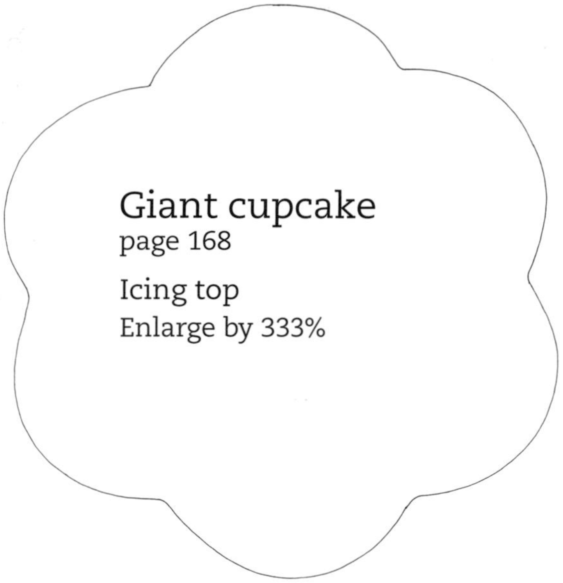

Giant cupcake
page 168

Icing top
Enlarge by 333%

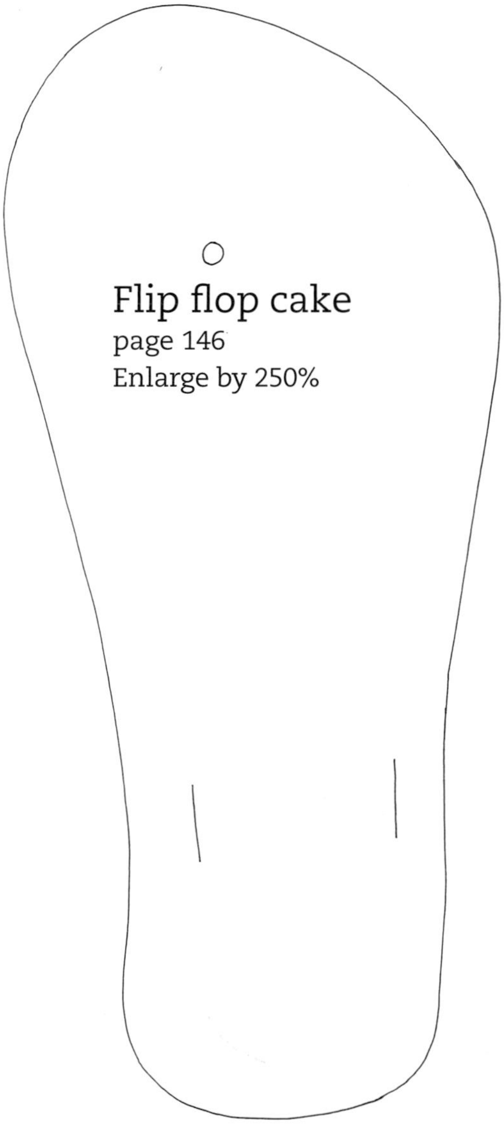

tie

tie

Briefcase cake
page 118
Enlarge by 200%

tie

Flip flop cake
page 146
Enlarge by 250%

Pirate cake
page 96
Enlarge by 300%

door

Rocket cake
page 150
Enlarge by 200%

wing

top

Paint tube cake
page 172
Enlarge by 250%

tube body

base size

Boat cake
page 114
Enlarge by 200%

top size

Handbag cake
page 178
Enlarge by 250%

side trim

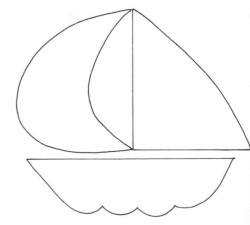

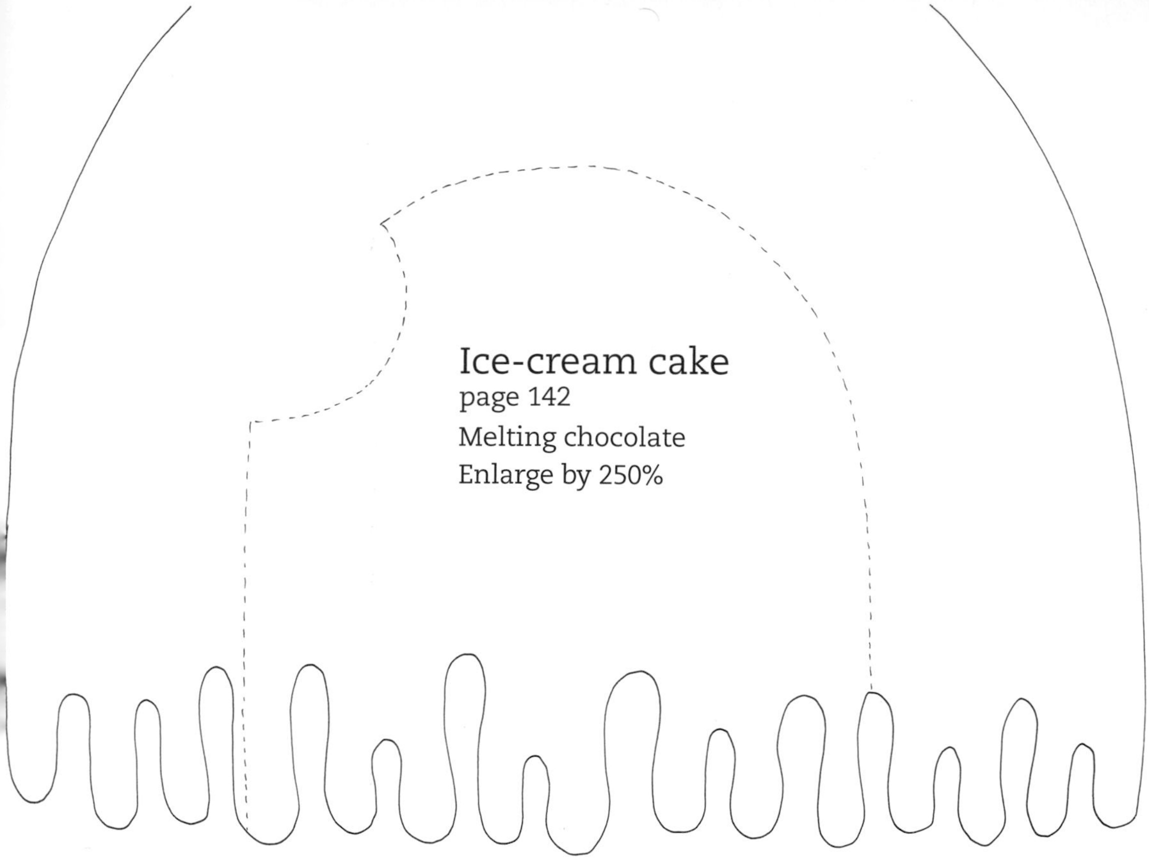

Ice-cream cake
page 142

Melting chocolate
Enlarge by 250%

Record player cake
page 126

Indentation for the record player

Actual size

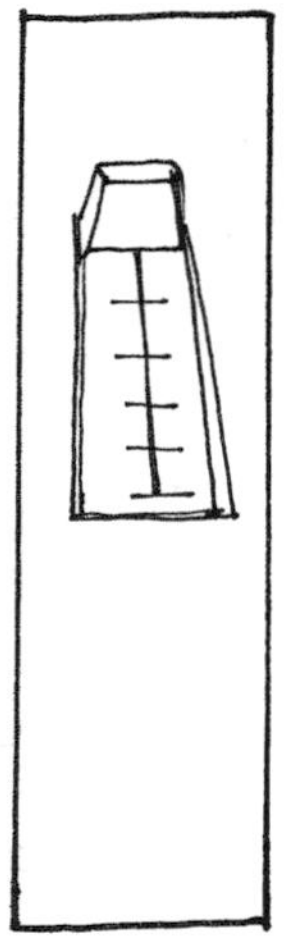

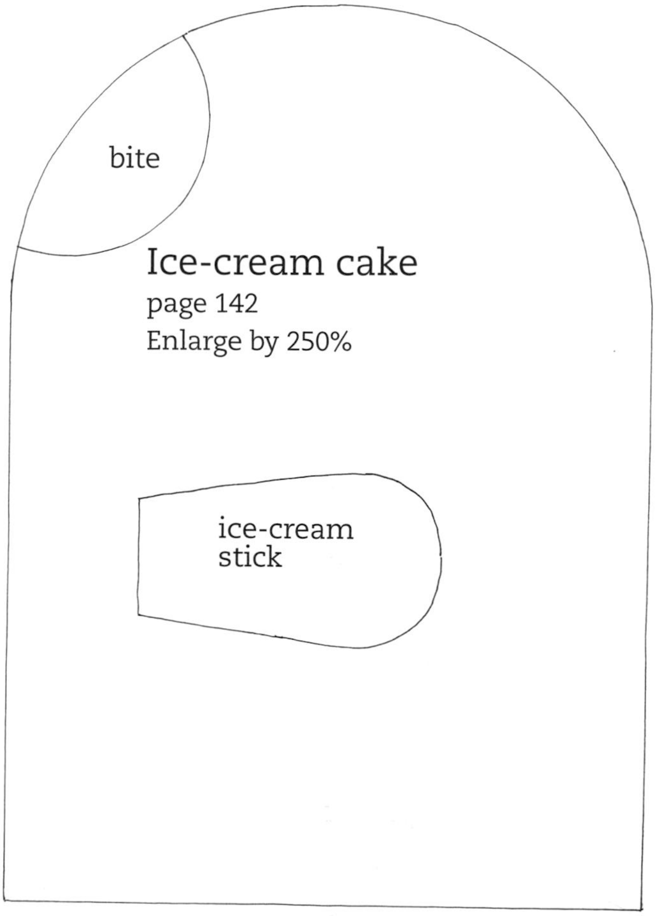

bite

Ice-cream cake
page 142
Enlarge by 250%

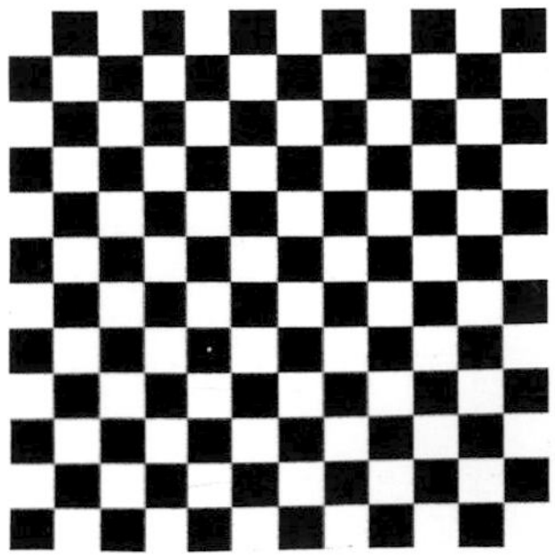

ice-cream stick

Racing car cake
page 92
Enlarge by 200%

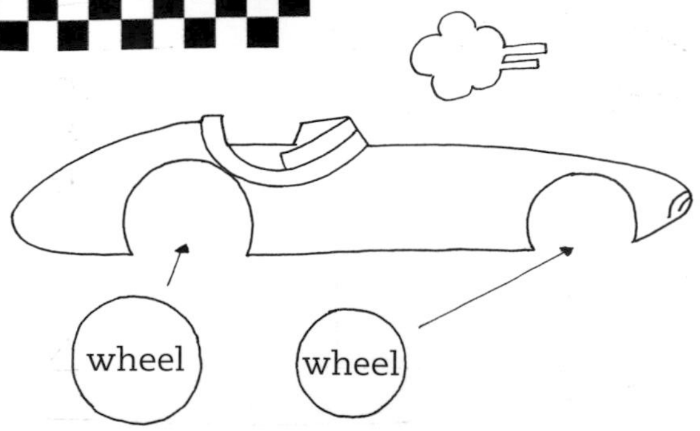

wheel

wheel

Index

Published in 2009 by Murdoch Books Pty Limited.

Murdoch Books Australia
Pier 8/9, 23 Hickson Road
Millers Point NSW 2000
Phone: +61 (0) 2 8220 2000
Fax: +61 (0) 2 8220 2558
www.murdochbooks.com.au

Murdoch Books UK Limited
Erico House, 6th Floor
93–99 Upper Richmond Road
Putney, London SW15 2TG
Phone: +44 (0) 20 8785 5995
Fax: +44 (0) 20 8785 5985
www.murdochbooks.co.uk

Chief Executive: Juliet Rogers
Publishing Director: Kay Scarlett
Publisher: Jane Lawson

Project Manager: Kristin Buesing
Editors: Kristin Buesing, Glenda Downing
Design: Marylouise Brammer
Photographer: Natasha Milne
Stylist: Kate Brown
Illustrator: Margaret Carter
Production: Kita George

National Library of Australia Cataloguing-in-Publication data
   Cutler, Paris/Planet cake. Includes index. ISBN 978 1 74196 318 2 (pbk.)
   Cake decorating--Amateurs' manuals. 641.86539

A catalogue record for this book is available from the British Library.

Colour separation by Colour Chiefs Pty Ltd, Brisbane, Australia.
PRINTED IN CHINA. Reprinted in 2009 (four times), 2010.

IMPORTANT: Those who might be at risk from the effects of salmonella poisoning (the elderly, pregnant women, young children and those suffering from immune deficiency diseases) should consult their doctor with any concerns about eating raw eggs.

OVEN GUIDE: You may find cooking times vary depending on the oven you are using. For fan-forced ovens, as a general rule, set the oven temperature to 20°C (35°F) lower than indicated in the recipe.